do it **NOW** *do it* **FAST** *do it* **RIGHT**®

Patios
and Walkways

do it **NOW** *do it* **FAST** *do it* **RIGHT**®

Patios
and Walkways

The Taunton Press

The Taunton Press
Inspiration for hands-on living®

The Taunton Press, Inc., 63 South Main Street, PO Box 5506, Newtown, CT 06470-5506

e-mail: tp@taunton.com

WRITER: Rich Binsacca

PROJECT MANAGER: Robert J. Dolezal

SERIES DESIGN: Lori Wendin

LAYOUT: Barbara K. Dolezal

ILLUSTRATOR: Charles Lockhart, Lockhart Art & Design

PHOTOSHOP ARTIST: Jerry Bates

COPY EDITOR: Victoria Cebalo Irwin

LIBRARY OF CONGRESS CATALOGING-IN-PUBLICATION DATA
Patios and walkways.
       p. cm. -- (Do it now/do it fast/do it right)
  ISBN-13: 978-1-56158-723-0
  ISBN-10: 1-56158-723-0
  1. Patios--Design and construction--Amateurs' manuals. 2. Garden walks--Design and construction--Amateurs' manuals.
  3. Do it yourself work. I. Title: Patios and walkways. II. Series.
  TH4970.P3725 2004
  690'.893--dc22
                                    2004019332

Printed in the United States of America
10 9 8

Acknowledgments

W e're grateful to the homeowners, businesses, workers, consultants, associations, and experts whose talent and hard work helped make this book possible. Thanks to Jack and Judy LeWinter, Barbara Lewis, the James Sartor family, Jamie Coleman, Allan Block®, Belgard/Oldcastle APG, Brickform, G.I. Designs, Nightscaping, and Petals Florists.

Contents

Patio and Walkway PROJECTS

Main Entry Makeover **22**
Give your home **A GRAND ENTRANCE** with a new walkway fashioned from precast-concrete pavers

Step Upgrade **32**
Try these tricks to **TRANSFORM YOUR OLD STEPS** so they'll stand the test of time

Stacked-Block Raised Bed **42**
Use **INTERLOCKING BLOCKS** to build a raised bed for your annual and perennial flowers, a birdbath, or a tree

BBQ Headquarters **52**
Give yourself (and your grill) a stage worthy of a backyard gourmet with a **PERFECT PATIO** of precast pavers

How to Use This Book

I F YOU'RE INTERESTED IN HOME IMPROVEMENTS that add value and convenience while also enabling you to express your own sense of style, you've come to the right place. **Do It Now/Do It Fast/Do It Right** books are created with an attitude that says "Let's get started!" and an ideal mix of home-improvement inspiration and how-to information. Do It Now books don't skip important steps or force you to guess at what needs to be done to take a project from start to finish.

You'll find that this book has a friendly, easy-to-use format. (See the sample pages shown here.) You'll begin each project knowing exactly what tools and gear you'll need, and what materials to buy at your home center or building-supply outlet. You can get started confidently because every step is illustrated and explained. Along the way, you'll discover plenty of expert advice packed into the margins. For ideas on how to personalize your project, check out the design options pages that follow the step-by-step instructions.

WORK TOGETHER

If you like company when you go to the movies or clean up the kitchen, you'll probably feel the same way about tackling home-improvement projects. The work will go faster, and you'll have a partner to share in the adventure. You'll

Get the TOOLS & GEAR you need. You'll also find out what features and details are important.

SAFETY FIRST helps you keep you and your project free of accidents and hazards.

LINGO explains words that the pros know.

WHAT TO BUY helps you put together your project shopping list, so you get all the materials you need.

COOL TOOL puts you in touch with tools that make the job easier.

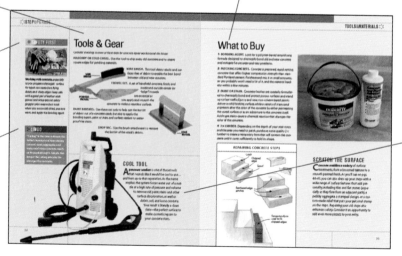

Basic Tool Set

Every home should have a basic set of tools that serves a variety of needs, from day-to-day maintenance to one-time projects. In a few instances, you'll want to rent rather than buy a particular tool for a specific task. Consider the following tools and equipment to help make your patio and path dreams a reality:

SHOVELS. One flat-edged and one pointed-edged (or spade) shovel address almost any light digging needs and help transfer loose materials from cart to site.

STEEL GARDEN RAKE. Use this tool for spreading soil, gravel, aggregate, and sand.

HAND TAMPER. Use this flat-faced tool with or without padding to compact soil, aggregate, and sand.

PICKAX OR MATTOCK. Get either or both of these to knock out unwanted concrete and to trench soil. The latter tool features a pointed pick end for penetrating and a flat, vertical blade for digging shallow trenches and prying.

8-LB. TO 12-LB. SLEDGEHAMMER AND PRY BAR. Break up unwanted concrete with the sledgehammer and pull it from its soil bed with the pry bar.

WHEELBARROW OR GARDEN CART. Your choice, but the two-wheel design of a garden cart often makes it easier to handle heavy loads without tipping the contents or causing back strain.

MASONRY TOOLS. Have flat, pointed, edging, and angled trowels at the ready, as well as a float to spread and smooth a patch or other wet concrete. You'll also want a notched mortaring trowel and a foam-rubber-faced grouting trowel. A rock or mason's hammer and a cold chisel and brickset are required for manual paver cuts.

ROCK HAMMER

COLD CHISEL

HAND TAMPER

FLAT TROWEL

POINTED TROWEL

LEVELS. Have at least a 4-ft. carpenter's level for checking the slope or flatness of your work; a 2-ft. version is optional, as is a line level and a laser sight level.

BRUSHES. Use a wire brush to clear out unwanted concrete shards and dust, and paint brushes for applying bonding agents.

BROOM. You'll need a push broom for spreading sand between paver joints and general clean up.

SCREWDRIVERS. Keep a set of flathead and Phillips-head tools and bits.

TAPE MEASURE. The most common is a 25-ft. retractable metal tape, but 40-ft. retractables and 50-ft. and 100-ft. reel-style measures are also acceptable. These longer versions help take measurements along curved edges.

SHEARS. Have a pair of wire cutters and tin snips handy for cutting cable and plastic edging material.

CORDLESS DRILL. Obtain a drill with at least a 14-volt motor to handle mid-duty jobs, with a set of drill and screw bits and one or more universal rechargeable battery packs to accommodate future cordless tool purchases.

SHOP VAC. A wet-dry vacuum will handle just about any mess.

ACCESSORIES. Stock your toolbox with a string line, a chalk line, a few carpenter's pencils, a utility knife (with extra blades), and a rubber-headed hammer or mallet. Also plan to keep a 25-ft. garden hose, a sponge mop, and a large sponge handy for various tasks.

REEL TAPE MEASURE

TIN SNIPS

8-LB. SLEDGEHAMMER

RENTAL EQUIPMENT

Unless you're planning to go into the landscaping business, consider renting (instead of buying) the following tools as you need them: a mini-backhoe for excavating, a power turf edger to more easily remove a section of lawn, a motorized plate tamper to compact various base and finish materials on large jobs, a gas-powered cutoff saw or a wet-bladed tile saw and diamond-toothed blades to quickly and safely cut pavers and tiles, and a pressure washer to clean off stains and debris from paved surfaces.

◖ NEED A HAND?

Save your back by following proper lifting techniques: face the object squarely, center your shoulders over it, crouch down until you can grasp it as you keep your back straight, and lift with your legs, not with your arms or back. If the load is too heavy for you to lift alone—more than about 40 lbs.—get help.

PROPER LIFTING

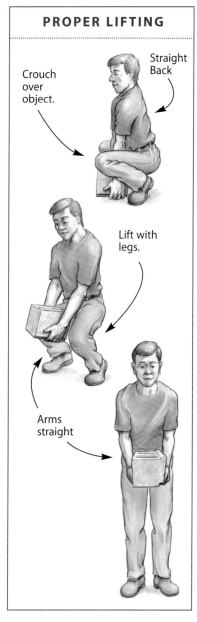

Crouch over object.

Straight Back

Lift with legs.

Arms straight

Safety First

A key measure of success for any project is walking away unscathed from a variety of hazards. Gear up for safety with the following items:

EYE PROTECTION. Get a good pair of ventilated wrap-around safety goggles that fit snugly and comfortably while providing clear view. Keep them free of dust, smudges, and scratches. If you wear eyeglasses, choose a pair of goggles that fit over your prescription lenses.

EARPLUGS OR PROTECTORS. Keep these handy to protect your hearing if you rent any mechanical or gas-powered tools. Disposable foam earplugs are one option; headphones with muffling insulation are another.

DUST MASK OR RESPIRATOR. Disposable dust masks keep your mouth and nose clear of fine dust and debris; buy them by the box. For heavy dust conditions and when working with powdered cement containing silica, rent a respirator and change or clean its filters frequently.

KNEE PADS. Protect your knees without hindering circulation with a pair of cushioned knee pads.

WORK GLOVES. Tough leather or Kevlar® gloves protect your hands and fingers from blisters and cuts as you work. In fact, you should never take them off until the job's finished.

WORK BOOTS. Steel-toed work boots are ideal, but the overall goal is to avoid open-toed shoes or sandals when working around heavy objects such as paving stones.

WATER AND SUN PROTECTION. Keep yourself hydrated with plenty of water or sports drinks. Keep your head cool with a brimmed hat, and lather up with a high SPF-rated sunscreen, even if the sky is overcast.

TAKE BREAKS. Rest often in a cool, shady spot or indoors and eat regularly to fuel your body for the next work session.

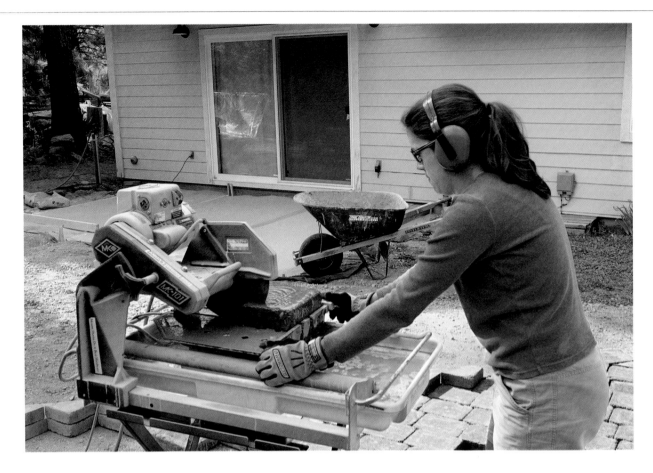

PLANNING A PROJECT

Even the biggest jobs consist of series of easy-to-do steps. Break them down into their logical parts: choosing materials, gathering tools and supplies, visiting a rental yard, preparing the site, performing the first installation step, and so on. What should you do if your skills are rusty? Seek out expert advice—most home improvement and hardware stores have knowledgeable staff who are happy to guide you. They'll explain what to do and when to do it, help you estimate how much of each material you will need, describe the tools you'll need, and show you which products to buy and which to rent for one-time use. Most stores will arrange to have your purchases delivered to the job site. Many also hold weekly seminars where you can learn the skills needed to pour and finish concrete, apply tile, set pavers, and perform the other techniques you'll see in this book. If you're still in doubt, practice on an out-of-the-way section before you move out into the main project. Once your hands are busy, you'll find things falling into place, and your work will give results you'll be proud of.

When using rented tools such as the wet tile saw shown, you will want to place your reservation several days before you need to use the saw.

Whenever you mix concrete-based products, make sure to prepare only enough to use within a 10-min. time frame to avoid wasting material. Clean and dry your masonry tools right after each use to protect them from drying concrete.

⊙ DO IT RIGHT

Every walk and patio project needs some sort of edging material to hold in place the edge pavers or bricks, maintain the shape of the courtyard or path, and keep adjacent turf or weeds from intruding. Look for an effective border control system combined with a look that complements the paving materials or that can be hidden from sight.

Before You Begin

Along with the right tools for the job and proper safety gear, adequate preparation for any project includes readying the area for the various stages of work and gathering materials required to complete the job.

PROVIDE DRAINAGE. First, make sure the area will allow rain, snow runoff, or simply water from a nearby sprinkler to drain off the surface and away from any adjacent structures, including your house and its foundation. As you excavate the area for a path or patio, slope it slightly (about ¾ in. every 4 ft., as determined by your carpenter's level) toward the lowest point of the yard, so that gravity plays a hand in your drainage plan. Maintain that slope as you add layers of aggregate, gravel, or sand, as well as the finished pavers, tiles, or stones.

STAGE MATERIALS AND WORK SAFELY. Besides providing adequate drainage, make life easier on yourself by doing what professionals refer to as "staging" materials. Simply put, this means purchasing and scheduling the delivery of your materials—from a few yards of crushed stone to a ton or more of flagstones—in the order in which you'll need them. For small jobs, that might be all at once, while for larger jobs it may mean scheduling the deliveries over a few days.

Place materials near your worksite, and make a trial layout of the paver pattern.

Staging also refers to placing your materials in close proximity to your work area. This saves time, effort, and the potential for damaging materials as you handle and haul them from one place to another. Protect turf and other surfaces by placing the materials on tarps or pallets, and never lift more than you can safely carry or move with a hand truck, garden cart, wheelbarrow, or your own two hands.

HEADY
DUTY LIFT
TRUCK

DELIVERY OF MATERIALS?

Not sure whether you should pick it up or have it delivered? Make your choice by following these guidelines:

PICK IT UP YOURSELF. Rely on your local home improvement or specialty supply outlet for bags of premixed and fast-setting concrete and patching material; thin-set mortar and grout; concrete paint, stain, or pigment additives; hardware cloth—also called wire mesh—and landscape fabric, or weed screen; stakes; 2× and 1× lumber for screed guides, temporary edgings, and corner boards; permanent edging materials; plastic sheeting; and all the fixtures, cable, and accessories for a low-voltage lighting installation.

HAVE IT DELIVERED. Even if you have a pickup truck or trailer, it might still be better to have suppliers deliver the following materials so they are placed properly and safely on your property: fill dirt; aggregate; crushed stone; washed pea gravel; pebbles; sand; and precast pavers, natural stones, tiles, and facing (or veneer) bricks. Calculate what you'll need based on the size of your project, allowing for waste and breakage (see Estimating Materials, p. 25).

Prep Projects

Make the job easier and complete it faster by **PREPARING THE AREA** for your chosen walk or patio material

A LTHOUGH EACH PROJECT IS DIFFERENT, prepping the area for whatever you plan to do is a universal requirement—and a critical one if you want the project to look good for a long time. First, you'll need to remove what's there, whether you simply dig up a patch of grass or demolish a worn and weedy walk. Then, you'll lay out the size and shape of your project and excavate to those dimensions. Finally, you'll layer soil, apply landscape fabric (to keep weeds from popping up again), aggregate, and sand—all compacted and level—to create a stable, durable base for the paving material you've chosen.

DEMOLISH   **LAY OUT THE PROJECT**   **LAY A BASE**   **LEVEL**

Shallow subsurface utility lines may cross beneath your work area. Excavate them carefully, then reroute the pipes or electrical lines at greater depth before you build a walk or patio over them. They should be buried at least 6 in. beneath your base aggregate or paving.

Make sure you have a clear path to easily navigate your wheelbarrow or garden cart when carrying materials, and make sure you can safely manage the load. Not only is an overloaded wheelbarrow apt to tip over and dump its cargo, but trying to control it can cause injury.

Demolition and Removal

1 CUT IT OUT. To get rid of a weed-ridden patch of concrete, use a rented walk-behind concrete saw equipped with a water-cooled blade to cut along the existing expansion joints to 1 in. or so below the depth of the concrete. If necessary, make a second, deeper cut. Take it slow, making sure you're staying on line and not lifting the blade as you go.

2 BREAK IT UP. Use a 8-lb. to 12-lb. sledgehammer with a 36-in. handle to break up the sections you've cut with the saw. Wear eye protection, leather or fabric gloves, a dust mask, and closed-toed shoes or boots to avoid injury from flying debris and blisters from the sledgehammer, and to protect yourself from a misguided swing. Take a full swing each time and break the sections into pieces you can easily lift and carry to a wheelbarrow or garden cart.

3 PRY THE PIECES. Though your work with the sledgehammer will likely loosen most of the pieces, a few stubborn ones will cling to the soil. Use a 3-ft.-long pry bar to lift and separate pieces of concrete from their soil bed. Keep your feet and hands a safe distance away as you pry the pieces loose—they can fall, crushing fingers and toes.

4 HAUL THEM AWAY. Even though the concrete pieces are small, use proper lifting techniques (using your back and legs) to remove and carry the broken concrete to a nearby wheelbarrow or garden cart and their disposal location. Once the big pieces are gone, use a rake to gather up the small (and often sharp!) leftover bits and carefully haul them away to be disposed of. Many waste disposers now recycle concrete, so check with your recycling center before adding to the load on your landfill.

A laser sight ensures square string lines (see Layout, step 2) and a precisely square area. The laser sight shown replaces the tape measure typically used for these tasks, making layout fast, easy, and more reliable than manual tools; as a bonus, it features a stud finder.

Before you dig, call your major service providers—gas, electric, cable, telephone, water, and sewer. They will identify and mark the location of their lines within the project area. Request that they use marker paint *and* wire-mounted flags to signal the location, run, and depth of any line.

Calculate how much material you'll need by calculating the job's total area in square feet—length times width—plus the depth of each aggregate or sand layer as a fraction of a foot. Multiply the area by this fraction to yield the cubic feet needed, or divide again by 27 to convert to cubic yards.

Layout

1 **CREATE THE CORNERS.** For layouts with square corners, use 2-ft. sections of 1×4 lumber to create corner, or batter, boards at each outside corner, at least 8 in. beyond the actual finished area. Nail two stakes to the inside face of one board, with one stake flush to the outside edge of the board, and pound the assembly in place. Next, nail a second board to the corner stake at right angles to the first board. Pound a stake on this board's inside face, then nail the board to the stake. Level the top of the corner boards. For circular or curved layouts, use a garden hose to mark the area.

2 **SET THE STRING LINES.** Use a laser sight to line up and pound nails in the corner boards at points marking the dimensions of your finished area. Tie strings stretched tautly between the boards to the nails on the tops of the corner boards.

Excavating

1 **START DIGGING.** Once you've had your utility providers—or their outside service company—mark the depth and location of any utility lines in the area to be excavated, use a flat shovel to start digging at one corner and work your way across and lengthwise (as if in rows). Try to maintain a consistent depth; pile your excavated soil and debris nearby to haul it away later (and possibly reuse it elsewhere).

2 **FINISH THE EXCAVATION.** Excavate about 6 in. *past* your string line. A carpenter's level is handy to make sure your excavated area is flat or maintains a slight slope away from the house, if desired for drainage; use a 4-ft. level to check your work as you progress. Remove any rocks, weeds, and other debris to leave a clean, smooth area for the next layer.

❖ COOL TOOL

A power tamper gets the job done in a fraction of the time it would take to compact soil or aggregate with a hand tamper, especially in a large, uniformly shaped area. Rent one from a local shop and wear proper safety gear, including gloves, to minimize the chafing from the vibrating handle.

Laying a Base and Tamping

1 ROLL OUT THE WEED SCREEN. Working lengthwise to minimize the number of pieces to cover the area, roll out the weed screen (or landscape fabric) and secure each section every 12 in. to 15 in. with 6-in., U-shaped stakes hammered into the ground. Take care not to tear the fabric as you go. Overlap sections at least 8 in. and stake the edge of the overlapping section to secure it and the fabric underneath.

2 ADD THE AGGREGATE. Fill a wheelbarrow or garden cart to a manageable level and dump each load of aggregate in a different location within the excavated area, which makes spreading it out with a rake easier and faster. Avoid snagging the landscape fabric, but if you do, repair any damage before covering it with aggregate.

3 SMOOTH IT OUT. To keep from snagging the landscape fabric layer below, use the backside of your rake to spread the aggregate over the excavated area, eyeballing it to an even level and consistent depth. Then use your carpen-

ter's level to check level (or slope) and a tape measure to check depth more precisely. Adjust as necessary.

4 TAMP THE BASE. Rent a power tamper to quickly and easily compact the aggregate base in preparation for the next layer. Start at one corner and work across and lengthwise. Don't rush, but make sure the tamper is moving evenly and consistently across the aggregate to avoid high and low spots. Check level (or slope) and depth, and add aggregate as necessary.

1

2

3

4

Leveling

1 **BUILD THE STRIKE-OFF GUIDES.** Secure an 8-ft. length of ¾-in. PVC pipe to a slightly longer piece of 1×4 lumber (see Do It Right, left). You'll need two of these assemblies, which you'll place parallel to each other, 4 ft. to 6 ft. apart across a section of the work area and 4 in. below the finished area's intended grade. Use your level to ensure the strike-off guides follow the slope (if any) of your excavated area, then secure them in place using 8-in. wooden stakes, a rubber mallet, and 6d common or duplex nails.

2 **POUR THE SAND.** Add a layer of washed sand on top of the aggregate base, whether from 60-lb. bags or by using your wheelbarrow or cart to haul it from a bulk pile in the yard. Ease the work of spreading it by opening bags or dumping loads in several locations within the excavated area, between the strike-off guides. Rake the sand to a consistent depth and visually level it. It's okay if the sand is slightly higher than the top of the strike-off guides.

3 **STRIKE IT OFF.** Use the straight (narrow) edge of a 2×4 that easily spans across the PVC strike-off guides. With a helper, move the 2×4 back and forth as you work it down the length of the PVC guides, scraping (or screeding) the sand to a consistent level. Work from each end toward the middle, moving the excess sand you've accumulated there to the next  section. Gather and remove the final bit of excess sand. When two adjacent sections are finished, lift out the guides, fill the voids left by the strike-off guides, and smooth the surface.

4 **WORK IN SECTIONS.** Narrow sections 4 ft. to 6 ft. wide are easier to screed than wider areas. Divide your work area into roughly equal sections. As you complete one section, move one of the PVC strike-off guides to the next location, level it, and stake it into place.

Main Entry Makeover

Give your home **A GRAND ENTRANCE** with a new walkway fashioned from precast-concrete pavers

A DMIT IT: THE PATH LEADING TO YOUR FRONT DOOR isn't exactly what you'd call inviting, much less a design element. Even if it's still in pretty good shape, you may just be tired of looking at it and wish it were different. With precast concrete pavers, you can take action and create a quick, easy, and beautiful makeover of that main entry walk. You'll enjoy ripping out the old concrete and preparing the base for your new path, then find out how simple it is to lay a new path of pavers and secure them in place. At that point you can step back and take pride in your handiwork—and wait for guests to beat a path to your door.

EXCAVATE AND COMPACT   PREPARE THE BASE   LAY PAVERS   COMPACT

A gas-powered diamond blade cutoff saw is great for cutting the walk edge in place and saves hours of time compared to a table-mounted masonry wet saw, but it has draw-backs. It produces enormous clouds of hazardous dust (wear a dust mask and warn neighbors to close windows); it's also loud and not as easy to control safely. Saws of both types are available for rent.

▶ **DO IT RIGHT**

The minimum recommended slope for drainage—along the length or, when that's not possible, side-to-side— is 3/16 in. for every foot of pavement. The maximum slope along the length for comfortable walking is 1½ in. per foot.

Tools & Gear

Complete instructions, including a tools and materials list, are available from your paver supplier. What's needed will vary according to the scope of your project and the existing site conditions, but this project requires relatively few tools.

LEVEL. A 4-ft. level will do unless your walk is narrow, which may necessitate a 2-ft. version.

TAPE MEASURE. You can get by with a 25-ft. retractable tape.

SHOVEL(S). You'll find good use for both square and spade types for excavating.

PICKAX OR MATTOCK, PRY BAR & 12-LB. SLEDGEHAMMER. Three tools essential for removing an existing concrete walk.

CONTRACTOR'S WHEELBARROW. There's lots of heavy stuff to move around.

STEEL GARDEN RAKE. Use this for spreading and leveling.

TIN SNIPS. You'll need a sharp pair of these to cut the plastic tubing.

TURF EDGER. This handy tool makes it easy to cut and remove turf along the walk's edges.

MASONRY TOOLS. You'll need a pointed trowel and a steel float to create a subsurface edge.

RUBBER HAMMER OR MALLET. This is the tool used to set the pavers tight to each other.

PUSH BROOM. The easiest way to fill the joints between installed pavers is to brush dry sand diagonally across the surface of the walk.

SAFETY GEAR. Don't work without eye protection, earplugs, a disposable dust mask, work gloves, and knee pads.

PLATE COMPACTOR. Rent a vibrating plate compactor to properly compact the base, sand, and pavers. Although it is heavy and might appear difficult to control, the vibration is managed with the throttle, and the machine moves along by itself. It's easy to steer.

HAND TAMPER. Use this where the machine can't go. Pad the plate to avoid chipping or damaging pavers, and tamp straight down to make sure the pavers remain flat and even.

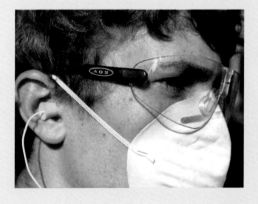

BE PREPARED

This is hard work; drink plenty of water and take frequent breaks. In addition to knee pads, which you will want when you install pavers, and work gloves, which you may never take off, you will need eye protection when breaking up a concrete walk along with earplugs and tight-fitting disposable dust masks when cutting the pavers.

What to Buy

1| CONCRETE PAVERS. Pavers used for walkways and residential driveways are 2⅜ in. thick and come in a variety of sizes; this walk required three different sizes to achieve the desired pattern.

2| CRUSHED STONE. Whatever it is called in your area—process screenings, Item 4, or simply crushed stone—make sure the mix varies in size from dust to ¾-in. pieces. It will eventually compact rock-hard over time, which is why it is such a good base material.

3| SAND. Order "washed concrete sand" for the setting bed that lies directly below the pavers and for filling joints. (Do not use stone dust or screenings such as Item 4 or mason's sand.)

4| PLASTIC TUBING. Use a length of flexible, ½-in.-diameter tubing or garden hose to define the edges of a curved walk.

5| CARPENTER'S PENCIL. Use a carpenter's pencil to mark the curve you'll cut along the edge pavers; maintain a sharp point with a carpenter's-pencil sharpener.

6| PREMIXED CONCRETE. A half-dozen 50-lb. bags should suffice for the subsurface edging and any handrail posts.

PAVERS ON SAND

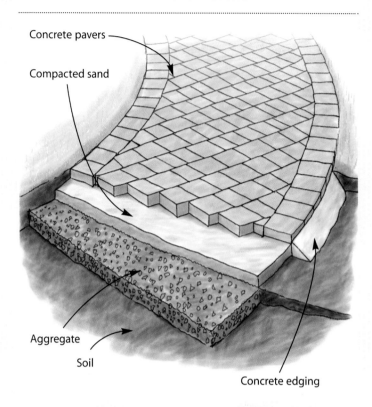

Concrete pavers

Compacted sand

Aggregate

Soil

Concrete edging

ESTIMATING MATERIALS

For the 4-in.-thick base of crushed stone, first calculate cubic feet: Multiply the walk length by its width, both in feet, and then multiply by 0.33. Divide that result by 27 to get cubic yards. Multiply the number of cubic yards by 1.6 to get the results in tons. Order about 1,200 lb. of sand per 100 sq. ft. of walk. Order enough pavers to cover the walk area (in sq. ft.) plus 5% for breakage and later repair. If the edges are to be cut, allow an extra 30 sq. ft. for every 100 linear ft. of cut edge. For the hidden concrete border, order a 90-lb. bag of Portland cement. Have all these materials delivered.

:: **DO** IT FAST

Wedge a stone under a large piece of concrete before taking a whack at it with a 12-lb. sledgehammer. It breaks easier that way. Wear eye protection!

▶ **DO** IT RIGHT

The cutoff saw was invaluable here when we needed to cut the concrete landing pad for the front steps and the paver edging stones. Wear eye protection, earplugs, and a disposable dust mask.

Preparing for Pavers

1 **REMOVE THE EXISTING WALK.** Use the cutoff saw to divide the existing walk into sections and to cut it away from the front steps, ideally along the control (or expansion) joints, if any exist. Starting at one end of the walk, use a sledgehammer and a pickax or a mattock (which has a point on one side and a wide flat part on the other) to break up the concrete and pry up the pieces. Carefully load the broken pieces of concrete into a cart for transfer to a vehicle for disposal or recycling.

2 **EXCAVATE.** Dig out to a minimum depth of about 8 in., removing all remaining pieces of concrete (careful, they're sharp!) and loose soil in the area of the walk, plus about 8 in. on each side, cutting turf as needed. Drive a stake to help gauge the extra width needed. Rake the soil level with a steel garden rake and tamp it firm with a vibrating-plate compactor.

3 **PREPARE THE BASE.** Using a wheelbarrow or garden cart, haul the crushed stone and distribute it in piles along the excavated walk area. Spread it with the steel garden rake to a 4-in. depth, or until the top of the base is about 3½ in. below the desired finished walk surface. Tamp the base using a rented plate compactor to provide a firm foundation that won't later settle or shift under the weight of the sand and pavers.

4 **PREPARE THE SAND BED.** As with the crushed stone in step 3, distribute the sand along the path and rake it level and smooth to a 1-in. depth. With a helper, use a straight-edged board as a screeding tool to level the bed and remove excess sand. Check for proper slope using your level. The end far-

thest from the house should be at least ¾ in. above the sand bed when the bubble reads level. Or, if a walk is level along its length, the sand bed should slope ¾ in. side to side (or "crown" in the center) so that water runs off to either edge.

Setting the Pavers

5 **PLACE THE PAVERS.** Position the pavers tightly against each other, using a rubber mallet when a little persuasion is required. Shift the courses as necessary to follow a curve or other changes in the shape of the walk. Leave an irregular edge on both sides, as you will cut those pavers to make a smooth edge in the next step.

6 **MARK AND CUT THE EDGES.** Use plastic tubing to define the curve along the edges of the pavers. Hold it in place with spare pavers while you mark the cut line with a carpenter's pencil along the tubing's inside length. Remove the tubing and cut along your line with a cutoff saw equipped with a diamond grit blade. Make a shallow (¼-in.-deep) guide cut first along the pencil line, followed by another pass that cuts through the pavers.

7 **INSTALL THE EDGING.** Place the edging stones next to the cut edges of the path, marking, removing, and cutting them to fit. Cut a 2-in.-deep trench along the outside of the edging stones for a banked-concrete edge, 3 in. wide and deep, that will contain the pavers. Mix concrete according to the bag's instructions, and shovel it into the trenches. Form a long wedge with a pointed trowel, and keep it damp with a sprinkler or a garden hose set on mist for at least 3 hrs., allowing it to cure properly and not crack.

8 **FINISHING TOUCHES.** Sweep *dry* sand into the joints and have a helper follow with the compactor, going over the walk again and shaking the sand into the joints. Repeat this a few times and again in a couple of weeks until the joints are full of

sand. Repair the soil along the walk with topsoil and grass seed, covering the subsurface concrete edge.

Concrete pavers can follow curves. Use edging rows (top), random patterns made with pavers of different sizes (center), and cut pavers (bottom) to emphasize the curved sections.

Concrete pavers offer a wide range of design options to create a front walk that adds interest, value, and style. You can vary the look of the walk to fit your personal taste or your yard's existing design by using a mosaic of colors, sizes, and shapes; or, for a more formal look, stick to one size paver, but use a herringbone or crosshatch pattern, perhaps with square edges instead of a curve. Install matching veneer (or half) pavers on the steps leading up to the front door to tie the design together.

Change levels in a concrete-paver walk by placing a cut stone at the point where the surface rises. You can also stand pavers on edge or end to make steps.

Common bricks have a pleasing appearance and are placed in a manner similar to pavers set on sand. A grouted joint makes the surface weatherproof, adding to its longevity. Bricks can also be mortared atop an existing concrete sidewalk.

Pavers come in all colors and shapes, so look over the selection carefully before choosing your materials. Choose colors that blend or contrast with your home's hue.

Step Upgrade

Try these tricks to **TRANSFORM YOUR OLD STEPS** so they'll stand the test of time

YOU NEVER GET A SECOND CHANCE TO MAKE A FIRST IMPRESSION. If the concrete steps leading up to your front door are showing unsightly cracking, spalling—the surface is flaking—or have other surface defects from years of wear and weather, consider restoring them. The only hard thing about restoring steps is repairing the concrete. With simple and fast preparation, patching, and finishing techniques and materials, you'll remake those old steps into an impressive entry. And you can use the same methods to make similar repairs to other structural and decorative concrete installations around your house.

| CLEAN THE STEPS | REPAIR CRACKS & SPALLS | SKIM-COAT THE CONCRETE | STAIN THE STEPS |

Working with concrete, especially as you prepare a damaged surface for repair, can create dust, flying debris, and sharp edges. Stay safe with a good pair of leather work gloves and wrap-around safety goggles; also wear a dust mask when you use a cold chisel, pressure wash, and apply the bonding agent.

▪▪ LINGO

"Curing" is the time between the initial chemical reaction among cement, sand, aggregate, and water and when concrete reaches its peak strength. Simply, the longer the curing process, the stronger the concrete.

Tools & Gear

Consider investing in some of these tools for concrete repair work around the house:

MASONRY OR COLD CHISEL. Use this tool to chip away old concrete and to create square edges for patching materials.

WIRE BRUSH

WIRE BRUSH. This tool cleans debris out of cracks and surfaces to enable the best bond to form between old and new concrete.

TROWEL SET. A set of handheld concrete, finish, and inside and outside corner (or "edge") trowels are essential as you apply and smooth the concrete to make a seamless surface.

POINTED TROWEL

PAINT BRUSHES. Use these not only to help get the last bit of debris out of a concrete crack, but also to apply the bonding agent, paint or stain, and surface sealant to water-proof the stairs.

SHOP VAC. Use the brush attachment to remove the last bit of a crack's debris.

EDGE TROWEL

KÄRCHER

COOL TOOL

A **pressure washer** is one of those tools that sounds like it would be cool to use… and lives up to that reputation. As the name implies, the system forces water out of a nozzle at a high rate of pressure and volume to remove old paint, stains, and other surface discoloration, as well as debris, soil, and loose concrete. Your result is literally a clean slate—the perfect surface to make cosmetic repairs to your concrete stairs.

What to Buy

1| BONDING AGENT. Look for a polymer-based emulsifying formula designed to chemically bond old and new concrete and mitigate future wear-and-tear problems.

2| PATCHING CONCRETE. Consider a premixed, rapid-setting concrete that offers higher compression strength than standard Portland cement. Purchase and mix it in small amounts, as you probably won't need a lot. The material hardens within a few minutes.

3| PAINT OR STAIN. Concrete finishes are specially formulated to chemically bond and protect porous surfaces and stand up to foot traffic. Epoxy and new, non-solvent-based paints deliver a solid-looking surface, while a variety of stains and pigments alter the color of the concrete by either permeating the cured surface or as an admixture to the concrete itself. Acid-type stains cause a chemical reaction that changes the color of the concrete.

4| 2× LUMBER. Depending on the depth of your stair risers and the area you need to patch, purchase some quality 2× lumber to create a temporary form that will contain the concrete until it cures sufficiently to hold its shape.

REPAIRING CONCRETE STEPS

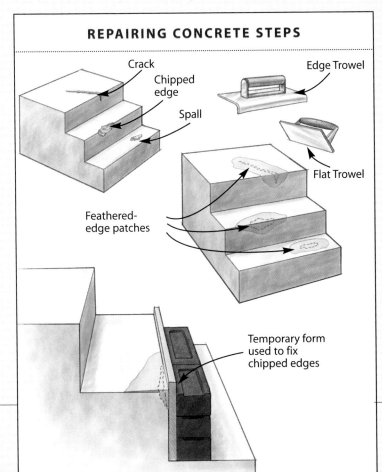

Crack

Chipped edge

Spall

Edge Trowel

Flat Trowel

Feathered-edge patches

Temporary form used to fix chipped edges

PATCH AND FORM

Wear, tear, and weather can wreak havoc on concrete over time, especially a high-use area such as the front steps. Cracks and flaky sections called spalls can be tricky to repair on the edges of steps. For shallow cracks, equip yourself with edge and flat trowels to form patching concrete along a step's edge; for deeper cracks, create a makeshift concrete form using 2× lumber set against the riser with bricks or stakes to hold the patching concrete in place until it cures. Make sure the lumber extends a few inches above the tread height, as shown in the illustration at left.

LINGO

To "float concrete" means to smooth it out and spread its outer edges so that the concrete lies flat to an adjacent surface; when you float a concrete patch, you're trying to make it look seamless against the existing concrete's surface.

Cleaning and Repairing

1 **PREP FOR PATCHING.** It's essential to thoroughly clean out a crack or other surface defect before patching it. Use a pressure washer (see p. 34) to remove oils, stains, and other discolorations; a wire brush and a whisk broom to loosen and remove concrete, soil, and other debris; and a shop vacuum and a dustpan to collect and dispose of any refuse—dust, chips, and dirt.

2 **SQUARE THE EDGES.** To avoid thin-edged patch jobs that can peel or crack on a flat or horizontal surface, use a masonry or cold chisel to create square edges. Make sure to remove all of the damaged area to the depth of the crack—without creating additional ones—to ensure that an old fissure won't get worse after you patch it. Moisten the area with water to prepare the surface for the bonding agent.

3 **APPLY THE PATCH.** Use a bonding agent to effectively and chemically adhere old and new concrete. Brush-apply the sticky, paintlike substance to the entire area being patched and a few inches beyond, taking care to protect your skin, nose, and eyes from exposure. Then mix and apply patching concrete, forcing it into the crack with a trowel and allowing it to overflow the patch slightly before floating it flush to the surface with a flat steel trowel.

4 **TAPER THE EDGES.** An angled (or edge) trowel makes short work of easing the patching concrete over an edge and molding it, such as from a tread to a riser. Gently float the edges of the patchwork over the existing concrete to create a smooth, seamless surface.

1

2

3

4

▶ DO IT RIGHT

Concrete cures in a chemical process and needs to be mixed in the right way to achieve the desired result. Follow the instructions on your patching concrete premix regarding the correct amount of water to add and when the mixture is ready to apply. You'll know it's ready when it is paste-thick, flows smoothly, and screeds and finishes easily.

＋ WHAT CAN GO WRONG

The cracks you're repairing now are likely the result of concrete that hardened too quickly, resulting in reduced strength and less resistance to the elements. To cure the concrete properly, mist it to keep it damp for several hours. Concrete cures best at a temperature near 73° F.

Skim Coating

5 **BOND THE SURFACE.** To create a lasting chemical bond between the old and new skim-coat concrete, brush the bonding agent onto the entire surfaces— top, sides, and edges of the porch and its step's treads. Be sure to read the package application directions and warning label regarding proper handling and health issues.

6 **MIX AND MATCH.** Concrete dries (or "sets up") and begins to cure quickly, so mix only what you need and can apply within 10 to 15 min. For small or low-volume jobs, use a tray to create your slurry. Larger jobs may require combining the ingredients in a wheelbarrow or trough, or perhaps using a power mixer. Make sure to mix your concrete in a place that can handle some mess—or take steps to protect it from wet concrete— but choose one that is near your work area. Wet concrete is heavy, so you'll want to prepare it in a spot close to the area being resurfaced.

7 **LAY IT ON.** Use a hand trowel to apply the concrete to a ⅛-in. thickness across all affected surfaces. When you are finished and the surface starts to harden, use a garden hose with a fine mist nozzle to keep the concrete constantly damp for several hours

to ensure that it cures properly and has long-term resistance to wear and freeze-thaw cycles.

8 **STAIN THE SURFACE.** To hide color variations between the original concrete, your patchwork, and the skim coating, apply a concrete stain using a paint brush or mop or paint the surface to achieve an even color and a smooth finish. Both concrete stains and paints are specially formulated to provide for penetration, adhesion, extra protection, and lasting quality.

5

6

7

8

Use a flat trowel to imbed small pebbles flush with the surface of a concrete walk before it hardens. After the walk has set, use a garden sprayer to apply cola soda to the surface; it will etch the concrete covering the pebbles. When the walk has cured completely, wash the surface to reveal the pebbles. The result is a non-skid surface with texture and appeal.

Finish a walk's edge with smooth concrete using a flat steel trowel; make joints with a jointing trowel, and texture the concrete in between with impression stamps.

Combine textures with concrete stains to achieve effects that mimic natural stones or bricks.

Concrete can be a stunning surface without

any embellishment, providing a refreshing and contemporary simplicity in its appearance. But that doesn't always fit everyone's taste or house style. What's equally great about concrete is that it's a perfect substrate for other finishes and design elements that can enhance its appeal and value—and that of your home as well. Consider adding a bit of your own personality to a set of concrete steps while also improving their safety and complementing the style and materials of your home.

A smooth border surrounding a field of troweled joints gives the appearance of cut-and-set stones. The pattern can be reversed to have a smooth walking surface with patterned edges.

A concrete path edged with bricks requires two pours: the first forms a base as wide as the entire walk, while the second fills the center and is as deep as the bricks and their mortar.

Random joints made with a concrete stamp and an edging trowel offer casual appearance suited to landscaped areas.

Stacked-Block Raised Bed

Use **INTERLOCKING BLOCKS** to build a raised bed for your annual and perennial flowers, a birdbath, or a tree

LANDSCAPE WALLS ADD A SENSE OF PERMANENCE and prestige to any garden, creating raised beds for flowers or holding back a landscaped hillside from a patch of grass. But building one can be an intimidating project. Not this time! For an old-style stone wall encircling a bed of annuals and a birdbath centerpiece, all you need are precast masonry blocks, a bit of muscle, and a few hours of time. Designed to interlock with each other, the blocks can be stacked and set securely in place without messy mortar, saving time, expense, and clean-up chores. In addition to containing a colorful attraction for feathered friends, the round wall creates a comfortable and contemplative place to sit and enjoy your garden.

| REMOVE TURF | BUILD THE PLANTER WALL | INSTALL A BIRDBATH | PLANT FLOWERS |

Tools & Gear

In addition to a round-headed spade, a flat-edged shovel, a tape measure, and a good pair of work gloves, you'll need the following tools for this project:

HAND TAMPER. Use this wood-handled, steel-based tool to compact and level the 4-in. gravel base that will serve as the foundation for your wall.

GARDEN CART. Save your back and avoid toppling a load of heavy blocks with a handy, single-axle garden cart, ideally with a removable back panel for easy loading and unloading.

CARPENTER'S LEVEL. Make sure each course of your round wall, from the base to the capstones, remains level by checking it with a 2-ft. or 4-ft. bubble level.

RUBBER-HEADED MALLET. Use this tool to gently but effectively knock your blocks in place.

GARDEN HOSE OR STAKES AND STRING. Use a section of hose or string at least 20 ft. long to outline the wall's circumference.

STAKE AND STRING. Tie a 4-ft. string to a center stake for tracing the planter's outline.

COOL TOOL

A sod cutter/edger makes taking up turf easy and efficient. Once you've outlined the location of your wall with stakes and string or a section of hose (see step 1, p. 46), step onto this steel-bladed edger with your foot and use a simple heel-to-toe walking motion to slice through the turf. Designed to cut only about 6 in. deep, this tool allows you to quickly establish the outline of your circular wall and roll up the turf inside its circumference so that you can start excavating the site for your precast masonry blocks.

What to Buy

First, settle on the style and size of masonry blocks you want, then work with the retailer to properly estimate quantities for all the materials you'll need.

1| PRECAST MASONRY BLOCKS. For this project, we selected 70 mixed-size stackable blocks in three dimensions, as well as 22 beveled capstones to top them off. Their hollow core makes the blocks lightweight, while a raised front lip enables them to interlock with those below without the need for pins, clips, or mortar, creating a slight setback (or taper) for overall stability.

2| WASHED GRAVEL. You will need about 1 cu. yd. of washed pea gravel, with stones measuring ¼ in. to ¾ in., to create a 4-in. compacted bed. This will serve as a firm foundation for the first (or base) course of precast stones and facilitate water drainage away from the base course; water otherwise would be trapped inside the planter.

3| FILL SOIL. You'll need 1 cu. yd. of well-balanced potting soil mix to nurture your annuals and support the birdbath. Avoid soft, wet clay or spongy organic soils that are difficult to compact properly.

4| CENTERPIECE. We used a birdbath that complemented the color and scale of the precast blocks, but any similar centerpiece that suits your style will do. A ring planter is also a good place to plant an ornamental tree.

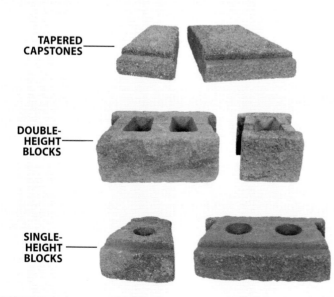

TAPERED CAPSTONES

DOUBLE-HEIGHT BLOCKS

SINGLE-HEIGHT BLOCKS

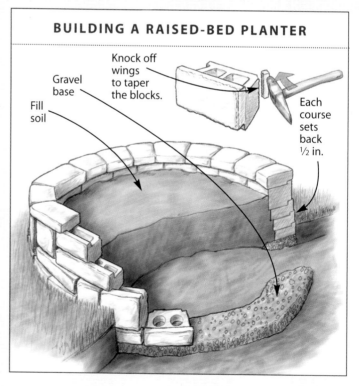

BUILDING A RAISED-BED PLANTER

Knock off wings to taper the blocks.

Gravel base

Fill soil

Each course sets back ½ in.

A brick tong enables single-handed transport of bricks or masonry blocks from the staged stack to the location of your circular wall project. The levered handle clamps the tongs in place, using the weight of the block to secure it, while the clamps adjust for small and large blocks.

For a retaining wall, you'll need to fill the block's hollow cavities and backfill 6 in. behind each course of blocks with drain rock. You'll also need to backfill behind that with soil to create a stable backing for the wall and to facilitate proper drainage. For clay soil conditions, also use a rein-forcement mesh.

Going in Circles

1 **DRAW A CIRCLE.** After you select a centerpoint, use a section of hose or rope, a string line, and a tape measure to create a perfect circle that will outline the dimensions of your stone wall. For this project, we measured a 3¼-ft. radius from the center-

point, creating a 6½-ft.-diameter circle. With your hose or rope as a guide, use your sod cutter (see p. 44) or shovel to outline the section of turf you'll remove before excavating for the first course of masonry blocks.

2 **ROLL IT UP.** Use a flat-edged shovel or turf-cutting tool to roll up the section of turf where your wall and raised flower bed will be. Cut the turf in small portions to keep the job manageable, and roll it with the soil to the outside to better preserve it. Look for other areas of the yard where you can reuse the turf, and use a garden cart to haul it to its new site.

3 **EXCAVATE AND ADD GRAVEL.** Secure the wall in the ground by excavating a trench 7 in. deep by 12 in. wide. Save some of your soil in the center for reuse. Partially fill the trench with washed pea gravel (see Building a Raised-Bed Planter, p. 45) to make an easy-to-level base for your stacked blocks. Use a hand tamper to compact the gravel to within 3 in. of grade. Make your way evenly around the trench as you compact the gravel to ensure a stable footing for the courses of blocks.

4 **SET THE FIRST COURSE.** With help from a partner, set each block of the base (or first) course snugly to the outside edge of the trench and side-by-side, removing "wings" from the blocks as necessary to curve the foundation (see Building a Raised-Bed Planter, p. 45). Use a rubber-headed mallet to gently tap the blocks toward their outer edges, ensuring that they fit tightly together.

Building with Blocks

5 **CAP IT OFF.** Use a carpenter's level laid across adjacent blocks to make sure the base course is level, tapping the blocks with the mallet or adding and removing pea gravel as necessary. Vary the dimensions of the interlocking blocks to replicate the look of a hand-laid stone wall, and top off the last course with beveled (or trapezoidal) capstones to create a finished look and a wall suitable for sitting.

6 **FILL THE VOID.** Spread clean fill soil within your circular landscape wall structure, compacting it every few feet with the blade of your shovel until the dirt is 3 in. to 4 in. from the top of the capstones. Settle the soil further by watering every shovelful or two.

7 **INSTALL THE BIRDBATH.** A simple, two-piece stone birdbath creates a focal point for the round wall that's certain to draw interest from friends and fowl. Make sure the soil is well compacted and not spongy or expansive so that the birdbath (or other focal point) sits steady and level and stays that way. Also consider burying a capstone just below the soil's surface to serve as a base for the birdbath. Test for level by laying the carpenter's level across the top of the birdbath once you've set it in position.

8 **ADD ANNUAL COLOR.** Surround the birdbath with a variety of annuals to showcase summertime color, offset the hard lines and monochromatic surfaces of the stone, create an even more dramatic focal point in the garden, and provide seed for the birds. Use the capstones as a wide, stable surface area to set your flowers as you plant them. Follow the planting and care instructions on the plant tag to ensure your flowers stay healthy.

5

6

7

8

Use interlocking precast blocks to build pilasters and columns, raised planting beds, seat walls, borders, or other features for your yard.

Interlocking, precast masonry blocks create a variety

of dramatic garden features, including planters, steps, patio borders, and attractive, low retaining walls. The varied shapes and sizes of these blocks enable an almost limitless design palette. Use the same-sized blocks for more formal gardens, or mix and match surface heights and widths for a hand-laid, informal appearance. In addition, the choice is yours when it comes to decorating your new stone wall, from a sapling or shrubs and flowers to a garden fountain, low-voltage lamppost, or even a flagpole—whatever your garden decor and personal tastes demand!

Terracing a hillside with multiple low walls yields a more stable and attractive result than a single high wall. A terrace also slows water, reducing erosion. Consider a terrace if you have a sloping lot.

While the ring planter demonstrated in this project is popular, building a free-form raised bed is another option. The result is more casual, and it complements the organic shapes of flowers, shrubs, and trees.

BBQ Headquarters

Give yourself (and your grill) a stage worthy of a backyard gourmet with a **PERFECT PATIO** of precast pavers

SAY GOODBYE TO THAT RUSTED, RICKETY BARBEQUE KETTLE sitting precariously on a patch of grass in the backyard. Today's tricked-out grills, and the cooks who use them, deserve a stable platform suitable for full-fledged outdoor cooking and entertaining. Here's an idea: install a backyard patio using precast concrete paving stones. Today's pavers come in a variety of shapes, colors, and sizes to suit your outdoor decorating tastes. And they install quickly on a bed of sand over gravel aggregate, making it simple to create a beautiful and durable patio you'll enjoy during cookouts for years to come.

EXCAVATE THE AREA	PREPARE THE SITE	PLACE THE PAVERS	INSTALL THE EDGE

◐ NEED A HAND?

A mini-backhoe makes backyard excavating a bit easier, especially when you have a large area to dig and wide-open access. Also called a "loader" because of its ability to lift and carry loads of soil and other material, a backhoe fits and turns in tight spaces and is easy to control, even for a novice. Rent one to save time—and your back.

✳ WHAT'S DIFFERENT?

Concrete pavers are a lightweight aggregate of cement and sand mixed with water and cast in many shapes and sizes. When put together they create many different designs. By contrast, bricks are kiln-fired clay and minerals, typically in rectangular shapes; brick pavers are simply thin bricks for non-structural uses, including patios and walks.

Tools & Gear

Beyond your basic gardening tools used to help with the excavation, gather extra gear to prep and pave the patio, including:

MASONRY TOOLS. To cut the pavers to fit the diagonal design, make sure you have a brickset, chisel, and masonry hammer handy.

TAMPERS. Rent a mechanical tamper to compact the sand base and a padded hand tamper to set the pavers in tight spots.

LINE AND CARPENTER'S LEVELS. The former will help set your string line level, while the latter confirms if your patio is level across several pavers.

PUSH BROOM. You'll need a high-quality, densely woven push broom to make sure your topdressing of sand gets into the joints between the pavers.

STRING LINE. A handheld spool of heavy-duty string will help keep your pavers aligned and level.

HAMMER. You'll need a 20-oz. hammer to install the U-shaped landscape fabric stakes and the permanent edging spikes.

WET TILE SAW. Rent a saw with a diamond-grit blade suitable for cutting concrete pavers.

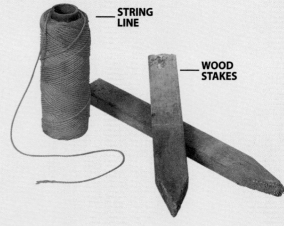

STRING LINE

WOOD STAKES

COOL TOOL

When you're working alone and want the job to go quickly and be accurate, a laser sighting device is the tool you need. Replacing manual tools, this battery-powered high-tech treasure delivers a dot or line of light to determine plumb, level, and square across longer distances than a tape measure or chalk line and with greater accuracy than a 4-ft. level or a framer's square. Use a self-leveling handheld model to establish a particular spot or mount the device on a tripod for a steady, precise measurement or mark. Some models also are equipped with a stud finder for multifunctional value.

What to Buy

1| PRECAST PAVERS. For this project, we selected rectangular concrete pavers measuring 7 in. wide by 9 in. long by 2 in. thick. The design of the pavers in your patio might require some of them to be cut, so order an extra 5% to 7% to account for waste.

2| WASHED AGGREGATE. For the 10-ft. by 15-ft. dimensions of this project, a 2-cu.-yd. load of washed, ¾-in. aggregate or pea gravel provides a solid foundation.

3| SAND. Purchase 2 cu. yds. of sand to cover the gravel as a stable, level base for the pavers, as well as more sand to broom into the paver joints to lock them in place.

4| LANDSCAPE FABRIC. Also called a weed screen, landscape fabric helps keep weeds from growing through the blocks. Secure it with 6-in.-long, U-shaped stakes spaced every 8 in. and tacked in with a hammer.

5| EDGE RESTRAINTS. Replace the temporary edge boards you use to align the pavers with a permanent plastic border set in place with 8-in. galvanized spikes.

6| PVC PIPE. Two 10-ft.-long sections of 1-in. PVC pipe will serve as a homemade guide for screeding the sand base to level before you install the pavers.

7| 1× AND 2× LUMBER AND STAKES.
You'll need straight, 10-ft.-long pieces of lumber and wood stakes to support your screed pipe and scrap lumber for batter boards, screeds, and temporary edge boards.

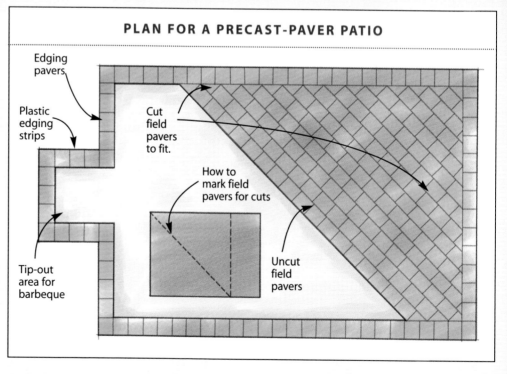

PLAN FOR A PRECAST-PAVER PATIO

Edging pavers

Plastic edging strips

Cut field pavers to fit.

How to mark field pavers for cuts

Tip-out area for barbeque

Uncut field pavers

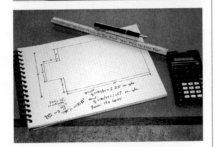
Preparing the Bed

1 **OUTLINE AND EXCAVATE THE AREA.** Transfer your plan on paper to its eventual location using a tape measure and batter boards at each outside corner. Pound nails into the batter boards and attach level strings as guides to the desired finished grade and outline of the patio's shape. Use a line level to determine a slight slope for drainage away from the house (about 1½ in. every 6 ft.). Measure all diagonals to confirm 90-deg. corners (they should all be of equal length), then excavate the area to 6 in. to 8 in. below the finished grade, following the slope.

2 **LEVEL THE PAD.** Use a rake to smooth the excavated area along your slight slope (as set by your string lines) and remove roots and other debris as necessary. Install a porous weed screen or landscape fabric, tacking it in place with U-shaped stakes every 8 in.; overlap the edges of the landscape fabric at least 12 in., and install the stakes along the edge of the top layer.

3 **INSTALL THE GRAVEL.** Use a wheelbarrow or garden cart to transfer and dump gravel into the excavated area, piling each load in a different section to make spreading it easier. Spread the aggregate out across the patio bed to a thickness of 3 in. to 4 in., but no more than 4 in. from the top of the finished grade established by measuring down from your string line. Make sure the grade follows the slight slope of the string line.

4 **TAMP IT DOWN.** Use a mechanical tamper to compact the gravel. Add more gravel or remove some, so that the bed is 3 in. below the finished grade. Use a carpenter's level to check the slope of the gravel bed across its breadth, width, and edges. As in step 1, set a string line across the area at a few points to confirm proper depth.

1

2

3

4

Work the Angles

5 **SPREAD THE SAND.** Use a wheelbarrow or garden cart to transfer sand into the gravel bed. Dump the sand in several piles to make it easier and faster to spread across the area. Roughly level the sand with a rake to at least 2 in. below the finished grade set by your string lines. Install and level temporary support boards 2 in. below grade across the patio for your PVC screed pipes to rest on, following the slope of your string line.

6 **SCREED THE BASE.** Attach pairs of 1-in. PVC pipes to the temporary support boards with pipe clamps (cut the pipe 8 in. longer than the boards). Beginning at one end of the patio, slowly but forcefully drag a screed board across the pipes toward the centerline, removing excess sand as needed. Lift the pipes and supports out, and repeat the process across the site.

7 **CUT THE ANGLES.** Pencil a 45-deg. angle on each field paver requiring cutting, and cut it with a wet tile saw. For jobs requiring only a few cuts, score the pavers with a brickset or chisel, and tap the scored line with a masonry hammer to break them.

8 **INSTALL THE PAVERS.** Before you set your first paver, install temporary edge boards using 1×4s and wood stakes to form a straight, stable edge. Lay all the outer pavers first, snug to the edge boards, then start the diagonal pattern inside. Stagger joints between the pavers, using a rubber-headed mallet to set them in the sand base and to narrow the joints between them. Check for a level surface with your carpenter's level.

5

6

7

8

Ready, Set, Grill

9 **WORK TO A CORNER.** Continue to install pavers one course at a time across the width of the patio's base, cutting the field pavers to fit against the edge pavers as you go. Make sure that each paver is firmly set (but not buried) in the sand and level to the slight slope you've established. Periodically check and tighten your string lines, as necessary to ensure the pavers follow your desired finished grade.

10 **REPLACE THE EDGING.** Once you've installed all of the pavers, gently remove the temporary edge boards by rocking them upwards, and replace them with sections of permanent plastic edge restraints. Secure each section of the edge restraints in place by pounding 8-in. galvanized spikes into their mounting holes. Galvanized spikes resist corrosion in soil or wet weather.

11 **TAMP IT DOWN.** Use the mechanical tamper that previously set the gravel base to lock the pavers firmly in their sand bed without risk of chipping or cracking their surfaces (see step 4, p. 56). Start at one corner and work your way back and forth across the patio, tamping each paver and joint to ensure that all the pavers sit evenly in the sand. Test the patio by walking on each paver and tamp  any that "rock" back and forth on the sand until each one sits flush to all the adjacent pavers. Use a padded hand tamper in tight spots.

12 **BROOM IT OUT.** Sand acts as the grout between the paver joints. Carry and dump small piles of sand on the patio in several spots. Use a stiff-bristled push broom to spread the sand across the pavers. Work the sand into the joints, sweeping it several times in different directions until you fill all the gaps. Sweep any excess into a corner and scoop it up off the surface, then sweep the entire patio one more time. Finish the patio's edges with turf or flower plantings, or by applying mulch.

9 10

11 12

The same techniques used in the project were used to make this pool deck, patio, and steps. Where the steps rise, pavers were set on edge and capped with overlapping pavers.

For informal planting beds, remove groups of pavers, sand, and aggregate and fill the area with potting soil and your favorite plants.

The variety of available concrete

pavers allows your imagination to run wild with colors, shapes, sizes, and edge treatments. The shapes afforded by precast pavers enable you to design square or curved patios or mix and match shapes and colors—all the while creating a flat, stable, and durable base for your outdoor cooking center, patio furniture, and potted plants. Of course, you can also go "old school" with cobbled pavers and wide-set paver joints (try it with a durable ground cover planted between the stones) to create an informal country patio that quickly looks decades old.

(Opposite) Define a seating area by laying a circular pattern of concrete pavers. The courtyard shown here is 12 ft. in diameter, large enough to hold chairs, benches, and end tables.

Change the pavers' pattern to define areas and outdoor rooms with different purposes. Here, a circular pad used for dining is adjacent to a passageway and deck suited for lounging.

Water drains easily through pavers set on sand. Plan to grade areas where patio furniture will be placed, so that table surfaces will be level.

Many precast concrete paver patios are set with tight joints. By opening space between the pavers and using coarse sand as a filler, the patio has a more whole feeling because the pavers and joints blend together.

Choose darker colors for paving you want to blend into plants. Here, multi-toned pavers help soften the look of the patio.

Designs with random patterns have a casual feel and are pleasing to the eye.

Streetwise Entry Walk

Transform weathered concrete into an **ELEGANT WALKWAY** to connect the sidewalk to your front door

I F YOU'RE LUCKY ENOUGH TO HAVE SIDEWALKS LINING THE STREETS of your neighborhood, the same plain concrete might also extend as a walkway to your front door. But there's no reason you can't transform that gray stretch to the door into a path of distinction. For this project, you'll learn how to create an entirely new and improved front entry by facing an existing concrete walk with a thin layer of stone tiles set in mortar. The prep and installation are simple, requiring standard masonry tools, inexpensive materials, and minimal effort and experience. When you're finished, you'll have a slate-tile walk leading to your front door, one that will be the envy of your neighbors and which will enhance your home's value.

PREPARE THE BASE   APPLY BONDING AGENT   LAY FACING   FINISH WITH GROUT

Call them veneer tile or half-bricks—they all mean the same thing: a full-size natural stone or ceramic tile, or a brick or concrete paver with a thickness of ¼ in. or so, specifically for use over an existing substrate, such as a concrete walk. By contrast, facing bricks are usually about 1 in. thick.

◆ **DO IT NOW**

Ask your tile supplier to deliver your load of stone tiles as close to the work area as possible, such as on your driveway or on the lawn (setting blocks under the pallets to protect your grass). This method, called staging by contractors, saves the time of hauling materials to the job site.

Tools & Gear

Consider renting the expensive tools and other gear you'll need to complete this project, but plan to include these in your toolbox:

MASONRY TOOLS. You'll need a cold chisel to prepare surface patches (see p. 36), a flat and a notched trowel to spread and feather concrete patches and apply the thin-set mortar, and rubber or foam grouting trowels to apply, settle, and finish the joints between the tiles.

MOP. Use a sponge mop to apply a thin layer of bonding agent to the existing concrete surface to better accept the mortar.

CARPENTER'S LEVEL. Make sure your level is at least 4 ft. long so that it can span several tiles and enable you to maintain a flat and level path during the entire installation.

SPONGES AND BUCKETS. Use large sponges and buckets of warm water to wipe away excess grout from the surface of the tiles and the milky film it leaves on the tiles.

CHALK LINE. Snapping a chalk line to mark the center of the sidewalk adds precision to the first course of tiles. The remaining tiles are spaced equally from this straight first course.

RUBBER MALLET. You'll set the tiles into the mortar with a soft-headed mallet.

FLAT TROWEL

GROUTING TROWEL

SPONGE

COOL TOOL

Small jobs require compact solutions. Use a small-batch barrel mixer that holds a single sack or less of premixed concrete, thin-set mortar, or patching concrete for mess-free uniform mixing in a minute or two. The barrel mixer has molded vanes inside that tumble the dry concrete, sand, and rocks and mix them with water. Just measure the amount of water and follow the package instructions for a perfect consistency.

What to Buy

1| NATURAL STONE TILES. For this project, we used slate tiles measuring 12 in. square and ¼ in. thick—so-called facing tiles that are lightweight and meant for refacing existing concrete surfaces. If you use 12-in. tiles, the area's square footage will equal the number of tiles you'll need.

2| TILE SPACERS. Use these removable ⅛-in. plastic wedges to maintain a consistent distance between the tiles.

3| THIN-SET MORTAR. Thin tiles require a thin-set mortar, a mix of sand and cement that creates a solid, low-profile bond between the tiles and the concrete.

4| BONDING AGENT. A polymer-based emulsifying formula is designed to chemically bond existing concrete with new masonry materials.

5| CONCRETE. For the most durable base use a premixed, rapid-setting concrete with a compression strength higher than standard concrete. Mix it in small amounts, as it hardens within a few minutes.

6| GROUT. An exterior-grade sanded grout will stand up to the elements; mix only what you can use in 30 minutes or less, as it tends to dry quickly. Choose a color slightly deeper in hue than the matching tiles.

7| 1×4 LUMBER AND STAKES. Use 2–ft. long 1×4 lumber and wooden stakes to build temporary forms when you taper the sidewalk with poured concrete.

FACING A CONCRETE PATH WITH TILES

Tile spacers

Slate tiles

Grout

Mortar

Existing Sidewalk

Aggregate

PATCHING CONCRETE 5

THIN-SET MORTAR 3

GROUT 6

❖ COOL TOOL

A wet concrete saw makes quick work of cutting concrete. It features an adjustable diamond-grit blade cooled by water supplied by attaching a garden hose to the built-in fitting on the saw. With the motor running and the saw positioned over the cut, turn a crank to lower the blade and begin the cut. When the blade reaches full depth, the saw moves slowly forward and cuts the concrete, usually along an expansion joint.

❖ LINGO

Your tiles can be set in a variety of interesting patterns, including basketweave (and half-baskets), herringbone, common bond, English bond, and many others. Research the choices as part of your project preparation.

Preparing the Foundation

1 **WASH THIS WAY.** It's best to pressure wash the surface to remove oily stains, grime, dirt, loose concrete, and any other debris. This will help ensure the stone tiles will stay where they lay in their mortar bed and withstand the rigors of foot traffic, freezing, and thawing. Stay clear of the spray nozzle when it's on; consider attacking tough stains by hand with a wire brush, as necessary, then pressure washing that area again.

2 **TAPER THE JUNCTION.** Because veneer tiles will be applied and would rest higher than the existing sidewalk, a new tapered section must be poured to prevent tripping. Cut, break up, and remove 2 ft. of the walk where it joins the crossing sidewalk. Pound stakes to hold scrap 1×4 forms in place, flush with the cut side-walk's edge and level with its top surface. Slope the forms  down to the crossing sidewalk, so that their ends are ⅜ in. lower than the crossing sidewalk's top surface. Mix and pour concrete to fill the forms, and finish it so that its surface is level with the forms. Let it cure overnight.

 **3** **BOND AWAY.** Help the new mortar bed bond chemically with the old concrete by misting the walk with water and mopping a thin layer of concrete bonding agent on the old sidewalk. Read all of the bonding agent's package directions, and apply it as directed so the mortar and tiles will bond properly. Work in sections, and keep the path clear of debris. While a helper mops a section of the walk, lay out groups of slate tiles to make selecting and matching easier. Set aside any broken tiles that you find so you can return them to your supplier for credit.

4 **MIX THE MORTAR.** Snap a chalk line the length of the center of the walk as a guide for laying the first course of tiles. Prepare the thin-set mortar a few gallons at a time to reduce waste; mix only as much as you can use within 15 minutes, discarding any leftovers. Follow the package's directions for the correct amount of water to add to the mortar powder, and mix it thoroughly.

While spacers are used mostly to keep bricks or tiles set in a vertical wall from slipping down the face of the wall (from the weight of bricks above them), they also enable you to obtain exact alignment between the veneer courses. Uniform grout lines are essential to a quality job.

⏵ **DO IT RIGHT**

As soon as you mix your mortar it starts to harden and chemically cure. To be truly effective and hold the tiles, it must be troweled into place, leveled, and set with tiles before it hardens too much to form a proper chemical bond. Work in small sections —the area of a single tile or two—to ensure the mortar (and later, grout) stays moist enough to bond properly to the concrete walk.

Setting the Tiles

5 **MAKE THE BED.** With a notched tile hand trowel, apply a ⅜-in.-thick bed of thin-set mortar over small sections of the concrete walk. Apply only enough mortar to cover the area of a single tile or two. Use the notches on the trowel to create a uniform thickness of high and low ridges in the mortar. You'll place the tiles into the mortar, space them, and set them before applying new mortar and beginning the next tile.

6 **SET THE FIELD TILES.** Carefully lay each slate tile into the mortar bed. Use spacers between each carefully aligned tile to ensure even grout lines (see Cool Tool, left). Leave the spacers in place until the mortar sets; remove them just before you're ready to apply the grout (see step 9, p. 74). When the tile is positioned, tap it solidly with a rubber mallet to set it into the mortar.

7 **CUT AND SET THE EDGE TILES.** Rarely will the edges of the underlying walk align perfectly with your tiles. Where the walk curves or a partial tile is needed to finish the edge, set it in place before you apply mortar, mark it with a carpenter's pencil, and cut it on a wet tile saw. Check the fit, apply mortar, and set the tile in place. The centered chalk line ensures that cut tiles on each edge are equal in size.

8 **CHECK FOR LEVEL.** As you work, check to make sure the tiles are level along the path by setting your carpenter's level on top of several tiles across and down the length of the walkway. Note any tiles that are higher than the others, tap them flush with the mallet, and remove any extra mortar that squeezes out. Check for level again after any adjustments. As you finish one section and need to mix another batch of mortar, thoroughly clean and dry all of your masonry tools and the mixing container before starting the process again (from step 5, above).

5

6

7

8

Grouting & Finishing

9 **PREPARE TO GROUT.** Remove the spacers as soon as the mortar has hardened and the tiles are set in place, but wait overnight to allow the mortar to cure before applying grout between the joints. Mix the grout in small batches by following the package instructions (based on an area measurement). About 2 gal. of grout can easily be applied before it hardens.

10 **SETTLE IN.** Spread the grout with a foam- or rubber-faced trowel, then push or "settle" it in the joints. Remove and reuse excess grout from the surface of the bricks. The ⅛-in. joints used for slate tiles are too narrow to need pointing—making a U- or V-shaped groove in each joint— but if you use veneer bricks, use a round-headed grouting tool to finish the wider, grouted joints. Scrape away any excess grout that results.

11 **WIPE THE FILM.** Let the grout set for 5 to 10 min. (following the package directions) before using a a clean sponge and lots of warm water to gently but thoroughly wipe away any excess grout residue left on the surface of the tiles. It's important to remove all the film—left on the tile, it will soon become permanent. Avoid disturbing the grout in the joints as you clean the tiles of grout film; rinse out the sponge often and refresh the water as necessary, to ensure a clean surface.

12 **THE RIGHT CURE.** Mortar and grout must be cured properly to gain their optimum strength and long-term durability. Use a garden hose with a mister or soaker hose to keep the path damp for at least four hours, especially if temperatures are above 70°F. String caution tape around the work site for two to three days to block foot traffic. When the grout and mortar have cured, apply a sealer recommended for slate to waterproof and protect the stone and grout. A paintbrush is the best choice for a small tile walk; use a mop for larger areas.

9 **10**

11 **12**

Refine the look of your tiled walk by cutting tiles in half and using them as an edging. Where the path curves, cut them into wedges, narrowing the end nearest the center of the curve. Lay the field tiles after all of the edging tiles are in place.

Refacing a concrete walk provides a variety of functional, durable, and attractive design options to suit your tastes and the style of your home and garden. Perhaps you want to play off the stucco or brick siding or stone accents on the exterior your house, or match the color of your clapboard siding or a dominant tree or shrub. If your house is informal and asymmetrical in its design, maybe a less-uniform path layout is in order; if the house features an interesting pattern, consider mimicking it on the walk to bring a sense of continuity to your entire landscape.

Stone tile facings applied to a concrete driveway dress up the paving and match the walkway (see photo at right). Dividing the driveway into strips allows you to plant turf or ground covers between the two pavement strips.

The same technique used to install tile can be used for large, thin, natural-stone facings. Since the pieces are random-shaped, allow more space in their joints.

Resurface a front walk by applying a skim-coat layer of fresh concrete, texturing it with stamps, and staining it with color using a concrete stain (see p. 32 to see a demonstration of the basic technique used to apply skim coatings to concrete).

Set thick cobbles and concrete pavers in mortar instead of sand. For these thick facing materials, the mortar bed should be 1 in. to 1½ in. thick, and each paver should be held by at least ½ in. of concrete.

Fill edgings of facing brick with insets of poured concrete. Define areas with different patterns, such as the basketweave bricks shown here. Light-colored grouts show off paver patterns, while dark grouts will hide them.

Driveway areas of paving stones crossed by walkways of bricks—shown here—or facing tiles accommodate both vehicle and foot traffic.

Precast-Paver Path

Cast your own stepping-stones by filling **FORMS WITH CONCRETE** and personalizing them with a wide variety of materials

I T'S EASIER THAN YOU THINK to create precast concrete stepping-stones for a garden path. All you need is a mold—perhaps just a hole in the ground—a bit of sand, some premixed concrete, and an active imagination to unleash your personality and create a useful, durable, and beautiful walk. You'll need to work fast, so get your ideas and materials in order before you start; take it one step at a time, however, and you'll be able to try different options until you hit upon the best solution for your tastes and needs. If you've ever seen stepping-stones with impressions and surface finishes and wondered how they were made, here's your answer.

PREPARE TO POUR	MAKE THE STONES	DRESS UP THE STONES	BUILD A PATH

⊘ UPGRADE

Place hardware cloth under your concrete mold to provide a reinforced base for each step, thereby reducing the chance that it will break or crack under normal foot and garden traffic. Made of welded (or often woven) zinc-galvanized wire, the mesh can be cut with shears to any size or shape. A hardware cloth backing also allows you to cast the pavers in one place and move them to another.

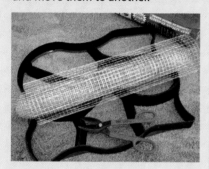

＋ WHAT CAN GO WRONG

Even quick-setting concrete must be mixed and allowed to cure properly to reach optimum strength. The mix should be the consistency of cookie dough. The concrete should be kept evenly damp for at least 4 hrs. after the mold is removed and before it is placed on the path.

Tools & Gear

In addition to a shovel used to excavate and place stepping-stones after they are cast, consider the following tools, some of which you'll use depending on the type of surface treatment you choose.

MASONRY TOOLS. Gather up a garden hoe, a flat trowel (see below), a mason's mixing pan, and a stiff-bristle brush (to use if you want to texture the surface of the stepping-stones).

HAND TAMPER. Use an unpadded tamper to compact the sand base before you install the stepping-stones.

TIN SHEARS. A good pair of snips will cut through your hardware cloth to create an effective reinforcement mesh.

CARPENTER'S LEVEL. Use a 3 ft. or 4 ft. bubble level to level one stepping-stone to another.

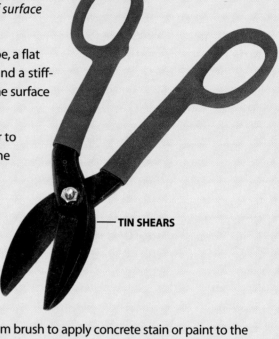

— TIN SHEARS

FOAM PAINTBRUSH. Use a disposable foam brush to apply concrete stain or paint to the surface after the steps have properly cured.

SAFETY GEAR. Always wear a long-sleeve shirt, waterproof gloves, a dust mask, and eye protection when mixing and working with concrete.

COOL TOOL

A **flat trowel is your best friend** on a project like this. Not only is it handy for smoothing out the surface of your concrete stepping-stones, but it also helps for tamping down and eliminating voids in the concrete that can cause cracking as it cures and afterwards, once the stepping-stones are installed. The tool also pushes pebbles and other embedded elements down into the concrete so they are flush with or below the surface.

What to Buy

1| HARDWARE CLOTH. Get a roll of corrosion-resistant, zinc-galvanized ½-in. wire mesh to add strength to the bottom of your cast stepping-stones.

2| PLASTIC SHEETING. Use a roll of 4-mil.-thick sheet plastic to protect your work surface, keep the stepping-stones from binding to it, and make cleanup a breeze.

3| QUICK-SETTING CONCRETE. Figure a premixed, 60-lb. bag for each stepping-stone; it just needs water, hardens in minutes, and cures in less than a day.

4| WASHED SAND. Get enough to make a compacted, 2-in. base for each stepping-stone to cushion it from the soil and permit good drainage. Sand can also serve as a soft edge treatment around each stone or to border the path.

5| PIGMENT OR CONCRETE STAIN. If you want to add color to your casting project, either add it in as you mix the concrete or apply it to the surface of the finished stones.

6| IMPRESSIONS AND MOLDS. Have materials in hand to cast the stepping-stones as well as those for imbedding in their surfaces before they cure.

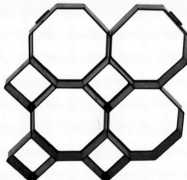

STEPPING-
STONE MOLDS

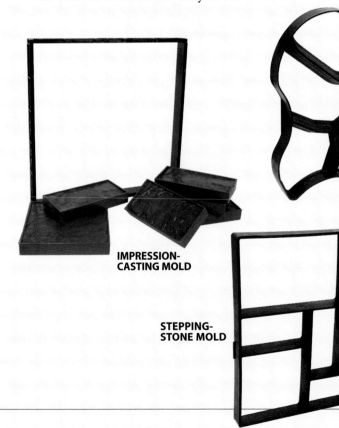

IMPRESSION-
CASTING MOLD

STEPPING-
STONE MOLD

CASTING CALL

Choose from a wide variety of molds to create the shape, size, and surface treatment of your precast concrete stepping-stones. So-called stamped concrete enables you to replicate bricks, pavers, cobblestones, or other surface looks, while preformed and custom-shaped molds mimic flagstones, square tiles, linked pavers, and every shape and size in between. Settle on one mold for your path, and use impressions to make each stone unique.

Casting the Stones

1 **CUT THE CLOTH.** Find a flat, stable, and open area, such as a paved driveway, for casting your stepping-stones. Cut out a section of plastic sheeting three to four times the size of your mold; hold it down with weights such as bricks or rocks. The sheeting will protect the surface below from the wet concrete. Use your mold as a guide and cut a piece of hardware cloth with wire shears, making it about 1 in. smaller on all sides than the mold. Place it on the plastic sheeting.

2 **MIX THE CEMENT.** Lay your mold on the hardware cloth, aligning the cloth and the mold atop the plastic. In the mixing tray, combine water and one bag of quick-setting concrete mix per mold. Follow the instructions on the package for how much water to add, and mix thoroughly, working the ingredients and water together by drawing a hoe from the tray's edges to its center. The mix should be the consistency of cookie dough.

3 **FILL THE MOLD.** Trowel concrete into the mold, filling it at least 1½ in. to 2 in. deep or to the top of each cell. Tamp the surface gently with a flat trowel to fill the edges of the mold, remove air bubbles, settle large rocks, and prepare the surface for further treatment. Work an edge of the trowel down into the mix at its edges to fill any voids between the concrete and the mold.

4 **LET IT HARDEN.** After applying the desired surface texture, brushing it, or imbedding pebbles (see pp. 94–95), gently remove the mold to allow the curing concrete to bond into a monolithic stepping-stone. Rinse off and thoroughly dry your tools and the mold while the precast stone hardens and begins to cure, a process that takes place after 30 min. or so. Keep the stone evenly moist with a continuous mist or light sprinkler for a few hours and allow it to harden overnight. Carefully lift it off the plastic sheeting and transport it to its final location in your path or patio.

Add a personal touch to the stepping-stones. Send a message with a famous quotation or verses of a poem etched into the surface, press cookie-cutters into the concrete, or honor a loved one with a memorial plaque embedded in the stone. You'll create lasting memories and leave a permanent impression to treasure.

+ **WHAT CAN GO WRONG**

Avoid making impressions deeper than ⅛ in. into the surface of the concrete—it will trap water. If the water freezes there, it will expand and could crack the concrete; even standing water can open tiny fissures that will degrade the strength and durability of the stones.

Customizing the Stones

Each stepping-stone can be finished in a variety of ways. Here are four popular choices used to decorate and personalize the stones:

5 **PIGMENTING.** Create colorful stepping-stones by adding color pigments. Available as powders or liquids you add as you mix the concrete, pigments come in many earth-toned or pastel colors. A single color gives a consistent path appearance, while two or three colors on staggered stones creates a more whimsical walk. Pigments create color throughout the entire stepping-stone without affecting durability or hardness. Follow the pigment label directions.

6 **POP IT UP.** After smoothing the surface of the stepping-stone, embed polished pebbles flush to the concrete with your flat trowel. Allow the concrete to cure until its surface absorbs the water that forms (about 20 to 30 min.), then gently pour carbonated cola over the surface to etch away the surface concrete, revealing the non-skid pebble surface.

7 **STAIN THE SURFACE.** Once the steps have cured overnight, apply a concrete stain with a disposable paint brush to add color to the surface while maintaining its natural or applied texture. Specially formulated to bond with curing concrete, stains also have water-resistant properties that enhance the durability of the stone's surface and extend its life.

8 **CUSTOMIZE YOUR CAST.** There are several ways to add your personal stamp to cast stepping-stones. For instance, you can leave a lasting impression by embedding leaves and twigs to create a textured relief. Or let each family member and your pets leave their hand or paw prints (no more than ⅛ in. deep). For a more abstract texture and a walk that's safe for

use when wet, use a stiff-bristle brush to create a crosshatched or other pattern. Mix and match customized stones for a truly intriguing garden path.

5 **6**

7 **8**

● NEED A HAND?

You can cast stepping-stones out of almost anything that holds a form, from a pizza box to a pie tin or a trash can lid. Or, you can simply pour the concrete directly into an excavated hole, with a sand base and hardware cloth installed, using the space to contain and shape the concrete.

Positioning the Stones

9 **EXCAVATE THE AREA.** Each precast stone will require its own excavation to embed it into the turf or soil. Press the mold down firmly into the turf or soil to make an outline of the mold's shape to use as a guide, then remove it. It will leave its impression, simplifying the removal of an area of turf that matches the mold's shape. Excavate the soil where the new stepping-stone will be placed. Its depth should equal the thickness of the stone plus an additional ½ in. for the sand base.

10 **TAMP IT DOWN.** Pound the soil with the unpadded steel base of the hand tamper to compress it and make it ready for the sand base. Make sure to remove all roots, rocks, and other intrusions that might push up or break the stepping-stone from underneath.

11 **ADD THE SAND.** A sand base at least ½ in. deep is essential to help embed and stabilize each stone in its excavated area, as well as to provide a cushion from the soil and to facilitate proper moisture and water drainage away from the underside of the concrete. Spread the sand, then compact it with the hand tamper to achieve the proper depth so that the stepping-stone will be flush to the finished grade. Use a mist nozzle on your garden hose to slightly moisten the sand before placing each stone.

12 **INSTALL AND LEVEL THE STONES.** Gently set the stone on the sand base; it should fit snugly in the excavated area outlined by the mold (see step 9). Use a carpenter's level across two or more stones to confirm they are level, and fill in or remove sand as necessary to make sure the stones are resting flat and stable on the sand. If you like, add more sand around the edges of the stones to secure them in  place and provide even better drainage away from the concrete, or consider another edging material to complete the path.

9 **10**

11 **12**

Break old plates and imbed them in the wet concrete of a stepping-stone, or use rubber stamps with concrete paint and stain to make colorful impressions. The stepping-stones will dress up a gravel path.

Many different varieties of cast stepping-stones are available at home centers, garden stores, and nurseries.

Take old cushions, rub a light layer of petroleum jelly on them, and apply plaster of Paris to make a mold. When the plaster is hard, remove the cushion from the mold and pour cement into it; the result are stepping-stones that faithfully reproduce the cushion's fabric and shape.

The best thing about casting stepping-stones for your own garden path or patio is that you can easily customize and personalize them—it's a cinch to swap them out if you want a change of pace or a few happen to chip, crack, or break after several years of use. Whether you use a manufactured form or a homemade mold, the ability to choose shapes, add texture and color, imprint the stones, or even to add personalized messages allows you to create a truly unique walk through your yard.

Cut irregular shapes into the soil with a shovel and fill the excavated areas with concrete. Use a flat trowel or a concrete impression mold to texture the surface, leaving it rough enough to ensure good traction.

Cast-in-place stepping-stones create a neat finished edge for raised decks, allowing easy access for deck maintenance.

Casual Courtyard

Bring rustic beauty and informal charm to your garden with a courtyard made from **FLAGSTONE AND POLISHED STONES**

IMAGINE A PLACE WHERE YOU CAN ENJOY THE BEAUTY of the outdoors, gazing upon your garden as you sip a cool beverage, listening to the game on the radio, and keeping an eye on the kids. A courtyard creates that nirvana, whatever your version of it may be. For this project, we've created an irregular-shaped courtyard featuring flagstones and smooth pebbles to complement an informal setting. Set on a compacted-gravel base, the courtyard is not only stable but simple to construct; with a hidden edge treatment, it eases into the yard to provide the perfect transition from the garden to your home, with convenient access to both.

EXCAVATE   PREPARE THE BED   INSTALL FLAGSTONES   FINISH THE JOINTS

▶ **DO IT RIGHT**

To calculate the amount of sand, gravel, flagstones, and pebbles you will need, multiply the width and length of the area to get the square footage; multiply that number by the depth of the material as a fraction of a foot (for instance, a 3-in. gravel base is ¼ ft.) to determine its cubic footage; then divide by 27 to calculate cubic yards for bulk material deliveries.

■ **LINGO**

Flagstones generally refer to natural stones that measure at least 24 in. across and 1½ in. deep, allowing them to be placed on a dry sand or a level soil bed suitable for heavy foot traffic and other loads.

◆ **COOL TOOL**

Power turf removers are available at rental yards. They are tiller-sized machines with adjustable cutting heads that lift lawn turf from the soil, leaving its roots intact. Once the turf is cut, it can be rolled up for transport or disposal.

Tools & Gear

Supplement your basic garden tools, including a shovel, rake, and a pair of tough work gloves, with the following tools and equipment:

GARDEN CART. Use a two-wheeled cart to easily and safely haul bulk materials and tools to the courtyard's location.

KNEE PADS. Make sure they cushion your joints, provide enough elasticity behind the knee, and are tough enough to withstand rough stone.

HAND TAMPER. Use a 3-ft.-long hand tamper with a wood handle and a padded metal base to gently secure the flagstones in their bed before you install the pebbles between them.

CARPENTER'S LEVEL. A wood or metal bubble level measuring at least 4 ft. long helps ensure a level base and courtyard.

GARDEN HOSE OR ROPE. Use a length of hose or rope to outline the shape of the courtyard and provide a guide for removing the turf and soil layers for your base. Use either again to mark an area for your trial layout of the flagstones.

LAWN EDGER. Designed to cut into turf at a depth of 6 in. or less, this tool makes removing turf faster and easier than a shovel.

2×4. Use a straight, 6-ft. to 10-ft. length to strike off and level the sand base prior to installing the flagstones.

RUBBER MALLET. A cushioned mallet allows you to forcefully embed the stones in their sand base without the risk of breaking or cracking their surfaces or edges.

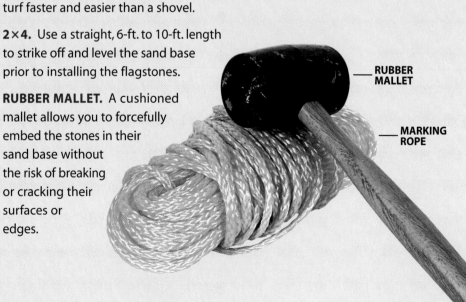

RUBBER
MALLET

MARKING
ROPE

What to Buy

1| FLAGSTONES. For this project, we selected 30 mixed-size flagstones, a multimineral derivative of natural field-stones. We included several large flagstones that will act as a level base pad for the table and the chairs.

2| LANDSCAPE FABRIC. A weed screen installed under the gravel base will block unwanted growth from below, easing maintenance chores and keeping the stones level. Make sure to include plenty of U-shaped stakes to secure the fabric in place.

3| WASHED GRAVEL. Divide the square footage of the patio by 6 to calculate the cubic feet of ¾-in. gravel you will need for a compacted, 2-in. base. It will form the foundation for your courtyard and help facilitate drainage.

4| SAND. Installed over the compacted gravel, the sand base provides a soft transition between the stones and the gravel; like a mortar base, the sand enables the flagstones to embed slightly and helps hold them in place. You'll need the same number of cubic feet as gravel.

5| POLISHED PEBBLES. Installed between the flagstones, pebbles provide a contrast in color and texture to the courtyard while solidifying the stones in place, blocking unwanted weed growth, and helping drainage.

Before you remove the turf to excavate for the courtyard, consider reusing it elsewhere in your yard or for finishing around the courtyard. The turf can serve as a patch for a dead spot, turf for a path, or as fill-in edging once all of the courtyard's stones and pebbles are in place.

✳ **WHAT'S DIFFERENT?**

This flagstone walk was built in the same manner as the project patio, but on a base of builder's sand mixed three-to-one with dry mortar. After the walk was installed, it was misted gently for several hours to moisten the mortar, then allowed to cure. Walks and patios built using this dry-mortar method stand up to freezing climates better than flagstones resting on sand alone.

Preparing the Site

1 **OUTLINE THE AREA.** Though an irregularly shaped courtyard implies imprecision, it's critical to determine the contours and dimensions of the space so that you can accurately estimate the amount of material you'll need and lay out your stones to fit that shape. Use a length of hose or rope to refine the final outline; avoid straight edges and sharp angles to create an overall shape that complements those of the stones themselves and results in a soft and easy transition from the courtyard to the rest of your yard.

2 **REMOVE THE TURF.** Using a lawn edger and/or power turf remover, cut along your outline and then carefully cut under the layer of turf, rolling it as you go. Cut the turf in sections to make the rolls easier to lift into your garden cart and reuse them in other parts of the garden.

3 **CREATE A FOUNDATION.** Excavate the area to a depth of 6 in. *plus* the depth of your flagstones, making it as level as possible and free of roots and other debris. Secure the landscape fabric with U-shaped stakes, overlapping each section by at least 8 in. Then, unload the gravel in small piles within the excavated area, taking care not to damage the fabric. Spread the gravel with the back of a rake, and use a hand tamper to compact it to an even grade with at least a 2-in. depth.

4 **INSTALL AND LEVEL THE SAND BASE.** Follow the same method to bring sand to the area, spreading the small piles with a garden rake or similar tool until it is at a 4-in. depth. With a helper run lengths of 2×4 or other straight-edged material over pairs of leveled pipes, and strike off excess sand from the top of the base to create a uniform depth and a level area, checking your progress periodically with a carpenter's level set on a board. Collect the sand at either end of the courtyard and remove the excess, then smooth it level prior to installing the flagstones.

Stonescaping the Patio

5 **PERFECT THE PATTERN.** Mock up the shape and size of your courtyard on an adjacent patch of grass or other open area to determine the patchwork of flagstones you'll embed in the sand base. Once you're satisfied, start at one end and transfer the

stones to their location in the courtyard. Working from the middle out, tap each stone into the sand using a rubber-headed mallet until it lays flat and is solid in its bed. Lay a length of 2×4 and your level across several stones to check and maintain a flat surface and the desired grade.

6 **BRING IN THE PEBBLES.** Once all the stones are securely in place and level, you should have joints 1 in. to 2 in. deep between each stone. Fill a small container with pebbles and pour them into the gaps between each stone. Guide the pebbles into the joints with your fingers. Check that each flagstone is held tightly between its neighboring stones by the pebbles.

7 **TAMP 'EM DOWN.** Use a rubber mallet to embed the pebbles into the joints and ensure a solid, level, and lasting patio surface. Use the mallet forcefully, but be careful to strike the stones squarely to avoid chipping and cracking them. It may be necessary to add more pebbles and tamp them down once the original pebbles are embedded in the sand.

8 **SECURE IT WITH BENDABLE EDGING.** Use the rubber mallet to drive galvanized spikes down through the joints of a concealed edging material to tightly hold the flagstones in place. Tuck the landscape fabric up at the edge and trim off any excess. Reuse pieces of the turf from the excavated area to surround and cover the trench along the courtyard's edge.

Flagstones provide a durable and beautiful courtyard surface and lend themselves to a wide range of design uses thanks to their irregular shapes and color variations. Perfect for formal or informal garden settings, a flagstone patio can be accented with a durable ground cover between the joints, a formal edge treatment, a raised flower bed, or a half-wall that highlights the edges of the stones instead of their surfaces.

Either dry-set stone patios or those made of mortared stones with grout have visual textures that help them blend into surrounding plants.

Border hedges along a path divide the walk from nearby flower beds. Prune the hedges to follow the subtle curves of the paving.

This small corner between house and wall is a perfect spot for a small, secluded courtyard.

Use flagstone of a single color set within a matching color of bull-nosed brick to make terraced steps. It's a design technique similar to the one used on the courtyard at left, but the final result is completely different.

Bull-nosed brick edging traps flagstones as effectively as a plastic edge strip. Its graceful curve helps delineate the courtyard from the lawn.

Rustic flagstones are part of the charm in this walk and courtyard. Pilasters made of concrete blocks faced with matching flagstone mark the entrance and support flower pots.

Stepping-Stones

Build your version of the **PERFECT PATHWAY** using random-sized paving stones

T HE RANDOM COLORS, SHAPES, AND TEXTURES OF FIELDSTONES softened by a traffic-tough ground cover create a durable and natural-looking path that adds a timeless element to any home. This informal trail gently guides you through the garden as if it were a meandering stream. It may seem to have been formed over time, but it took just a weekend to complete. With a variety of ground covers to choose from, as well as patterns to suit your garden's overall design scheme, you can easily create a bordered fieldstone path that will suit your life-style, climate, and decor, as well as to make a beautiful landscape statement.

EXCAVATE THE AREA **LAY THE STONES** **FILL AROUND THE STONES** **PLANT THE PATH**

Tools & Gear

___NARROW TROWEL

KNEE PADS. Save your knees from the strain and pain of kneeling on fieldstones with soft, contoured, and adjustable knee pads.

NARROW TROWEL. Measuring about 9 in. long and less than 3 in. across with a pointed, concave blade, a narrow garden trowel helps carve out the location of your ground cover plantings.

HAND TAMPER. Use a 3-ft.-long hand tamper with a wood handle and a padded metal base plate to gently secure the fieldstones in their bed before you plant your ground cover.

LEVEL. A wood or metal level 2 ft. to 4 ft. long is used to create a level path spanning wide distances. It should feature bubbles in the center and near each end so you can level your sand-and-topsoil bed before installing your stones.

RAKE. Use a metal-toothed garden rake to spread and level your sand-and-topsoil bed.

BRICKSET OR CHISEL. Use a brickset or a stonemason's chisel to score and cut fieldstones.

SOFTHEADED MALLET. You'll need one of these to gently tap fieldstones into the sand-and-topsoil bed and for cutting stones to fit (used with a brickset or stonemason's chisel).

SAFETY GOGGLES. They're a good idea no matter what you're doing in the yard but are especially helpful when you cut or chisel a stone and want to protect your eyes from debris.

TAPE MEASURE. You'll need at least a 25-ft. retractable tape measure to determine dimensions, so you can calculate square footage (length × width) and purchase the right amount of materials.

GARDEN HOSE OR ROPE. Use a length of hose or rope to simulate your path on a flat surface near the path's actual site, designing the layout pattern before setting the fieldstones in the bed.

MISTER OR GENTLE-SPRAY NOZZLE. Plants need a gentle touch. Attach one of these to your garden hose to avoid exposing the roots of your ground cover and the edges of your fieldstones during watering.

COOL TOOL

A **garden cart is essential for safely** transporting fieldstones, each piece of which can weigh 50 lbs. or more. Axled wheels provide strength and proper balance for heavy loads, while a removable side panel allows you to easily slide the stones in and out. Make sure to check the weight-load restrictions for the cart, as they can vary by size and construction.

What to Buy

This project has a short shopping list, though it's important to properly estimate the quantities you'll need.

1| TOPSOIL. A yard of topsoil typically covers about 108 sq. ft. at a 4-in. depth; you'll be mixing it with an equal amount of sand. Calculate the amount you'll need based on the surface area of your path, then divide it by two to arrive at the amount of topsoil to order. Have it delivered or drop it as close to the location of the path as possible, ideally on a concrete surface or on a lawn or garden tarp.

2| SAND. Like topsoil, a yard of builder's sand covers about 108 sq. ft. at a 4-in. depth (a single 60-lb. bag generally covers only 3 sq. ft.). Order the same amount of sand as you do top-soil. If you can get a supplier to premix the topsoil and sand, you can have it delivered in one load; otherwise, make sure the loads are dropped as close to the path location as possible and next to each other to make on-site mixing easier.

3| 2×4. Find a straight, 6-ft. to 10-ft. length to screed and level out your sand-and-topsoil bed and to use with a level to check that the bed is flat and even across longer distances.

4| FERTILIZER. Liquid fertilizer helps the ground cover develop roots quickly.

5| FIELDSTONES. You have a lot of choices here in terms of size, color, texture, and cut. For informal, high-traffic paths, select stones that are at least 2 ft. across and 1½ in. to 2 in. thick (steppers can be used for smaller and low-traffic paths). A ton of fieldstone at these dimensions covers about 90 sq. ft., but you'll want to buy 10% to 20% more than what you calculate to give yourself plenty of flexibility as you lay out the stones; you can use any leftover materials as a border in your yard or store them to use later for repairs. Fieldstone is available in lava, limestone, granite, sandstone, and slate—each with a distinctive color and surface texture, but all timelessly durable.

6| GROUND COVER. As with fieldstones, you have several choices of ground covers that can withstand light foot traffic, from tough woolly thyme to colorful creeping speedwell varieties and tiny, bright green rupturewort—even true mosses or mosslike leafy plants. Ground covers vary in terms of sunlight needs, eventual height, and ideal spacing; they should spread within a season so you can buy fewer to start and should be appropriate for the climate in your planting zone.

Laying the Paving Stones

1 **EXCAVATE THE PATH.** Once you've determined the general course and size of your path, dig out the area (including turf and other material) to its desired width and length and to a depth of at least 6 in. (or to 8 in. in freezing climates). Check level with your 2×4 and level and add or spread soil as necessary to take out any high or low spots. Pile or haul excavated soil and turf to an out-of-the-way location, compost pile, or elsewhere in the yard where it can be reused.

2 **MIX AND INSTALL THE SAND AND TOPSOIL BED.** Mix equal parts of sand and topsoil in a garden cart or wheelbarrow. Spread and level the mix with a shovel and rake, and screed with a 2×4 to a flat, level surface no deeper than your thickest fieldstone to ensure that your finished path will be level with the existing grade. Check level at several places on the path across its width and length, using the 2×4 and level together to span and check the longest distances possible.

3 **SET THE STONES.** Lay out all of the stones on a nearby site. Choose each stone by comparing its size and shape to the space you will fill. Lift stones carefully to prevent injury; they are heavy. Set, check, and gently tap each stone into the sand-and-topsoil bed, and then check that the stones are level to each other and to your finished or desired grade. Make sure each stone is set solidly (doesn't rock) in its bed to avoid breaking or chipping under foot traffic. You may have to lift a stone, refill beneath it, and reset it.

4 **BACKFILL THE EDGES AND JOINTS.** Use remaining topsoil without sand to fill in around the edges and between the fieldstones in preparation for planting the ground cover. Broom the topsoil over the path and stones, then use a padded hand tamper to secure the stones and firm the soil. Water the area to encourage settling, and fill any gaps with more soil until the entire path is level.

Planting between Stones

5 **REMOVE AND INSPECT THE PLANTS.** Ground cover should appear and feel healthy, carpeting each pack with firm and colorful foliage. Once you select the variety you want, remove a plant from its cell and inspect the roots; they should be firm and plump, somewhat molded to the shape of the pack, and with a healthy amount of soil exposed between the roots. A tight cluster of roots along the bottom inch or more of the plant indicates a root-bound plant. Make sure your ground cover meets your aesthetic and climate needs. Choose a steppable variety according to the amount of direct sun the path will receive; most ground covers thrive in full sun.

6 **DIG THE HOLES.** Use a narrow trowel to carve out holes for the ground cover along the edges of the path and between the fieldstones. Pay attention to the recommended spacing between plants indicated on their tags.

7 **BACKFILL THE ROOTS.** Use the topsoil you removed for each plant's hole to cover and firmly hold the roots in place in the soil. Use more soil to top dress around the base of each plant. Mix liquid fertilizer with twice as much water as recommended on the package directions, and apply it to the plantings with a hand sprayer.

8 **WATER THE PLANTS.** Use a light spray or mister attachment on your garden hose to deliver the proper volume without the force that could expose the roots or the edges of your fieldstones before they have time to settle in and take hold. Follow the instructions on the ground cover's tag for proper watering frequency. Keep a close eye on its condition for the first few weeks, until new growth appears, then water regularly as the grower directs.

5 **6**

7 **8**

Mosslike but broadleaved Scot's moss, baby's tears, or one of the true mosses makes a very low filler for a fieldstone walk. Protect plants from being crushed by grading the soil between the joints 1 in. to 2 in. below the level of the tops of the stones.

Fieldstone path joints can be filled with crushed gravel or fine bark, both of which contrast nicely with a mixed planting border.

Combining varieties of fieldstones and ground covers according to your own personal style and tastes means you'll create a truly unique fieldstone path in your garden. Consider mixing colors and shapes of stones, using a taller ground cover along the edges or even cut stones set more closely together for a more formal look and feel. Fieldstone paths can also connect patios of the same materials and design for a cohesive theme or be used to guide visitors to your front door or lead them to a pond or vegetable garden elsewhere on your property—all with the timeless beauty and certain durability of fieldstone.

Use fieldstones set into the lawn to make casual, low-use paths to connect areas where cut-across is inevitable. The stones will bear the weight of frequent footsteps and help keep the soil under the turf from compacting.

Use groups of four cut-stone blocks instead of irregular fieldstone to make geometric stepping-stone paths.

Connect low-use areas with narrow paths suitable for foot traffic but too small for garden wheelbarrows and carts. Small steppers are best for paving such walks.

Lighting the Way

Bring safety and style to your new walks, paths, and patios with **LOW-VOLTAGE LIGHTS**

ADDING PATHS AND PATIOS increases the value of your home— even more so when they're easy to see and use after the sun goes down. Low-voltage lighting allows you to showcase your handiwork after dark, highlighting your favorite features, casting dramatic shadows, and illuminating walks and patios for better safety and stunning beauty. Not only that, but low-voltage light fixtures are simple and inexpensive to install and maintain, requiring only your existing electrical service and a few components to create a lighting scheme that adds interest to your home and leads visitors to your door.

PROVIDE POWER **LAY CABLE** **ATTACH THE FIXTURES** **SET THE TIMER**

Tools & Gear

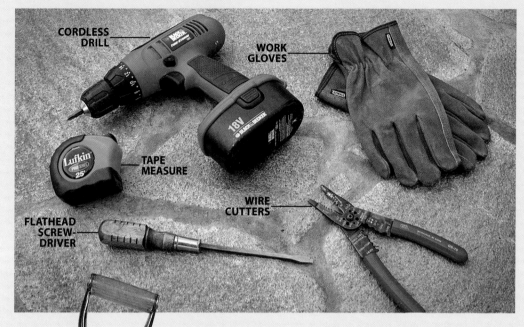

CORDLESS DRILL. Make quick changes from a drill bit to a screwdriver bit. Choose a model with at least 12 volts of power and 350 ft. lbs. of torque.

TAPE MEASURE. A 30-ft. retractable tape measure or a reel model follows the contours of your trench and gives precise placement for the light fixtures.

WIRE CUTTERS. You'll need these to cut and strip cable wires at the transformer and to make splices between cables that extend power to each fixture.

WORK GLOVES. Save your skin by slipping on a pair of these when you dig your trench and posthole.

FLATHEAD SCREWDRIVER. When you need a little more control over a screw, use a long-handled flathead screwdriver.

COOL TOOL

A narrow trenching shovel comes in handy for digging a deep, narrow ditch for the low-voltage cable and utility posthole when you're butting up against paths and patios. The long, thin, round-ended blade cuts cleanly through turf to the desired depth, enabling you to save and reuse the same section of grass to conceal your underground work. Look for a shovel with a comfortable handle and a steel blade for safety and ease of use.

What to Buy

STEP-DOWN TRANSFORMER

1| STEP-DOWN TRANSFORMER. This is the brains of the operation, converting (or stepping down) a 120-volt AC line to 12-volt direct current and serving as the hub of your cable run. Get one rated to handle the number of fixtures you plan to use and with a timer so you can program your lights for automatic operation.

2| THREADED SUPPORT STAKES. Attach these 8-in.-long, barbed stakes to the threaded base of your light fixtures as a secure anchor.

3| CABLE. For this project, you'll need a 100-ft. coil of 12-2 UF-rated 12-amp cable (a sheathed pair of #12 wires suitable for underground use). Most UF-rated cable can be buried directly without a conduit.

4| LIGHT FIXTURES. These low-voltage lamps are rated for 24 footcandles. Calculate how many fixtures you need and how far apart they'll be by their footcandle rating (see Lingo, opposite). For this project, the lamps are placed 6 ft. apart.

5| ACCESSORIES. Make sure you have T-splices, piercing connectors, survey marker tape, and a nearby GFCI-protected outlet (see What Can Go Wrong, p. 114) in a weather-proof housing to prevent shock hazard during wet weather.

6| UTILITY POST. You'll need a 3-ft.-long, 4×4 pressure-treated post with a beveled (or chamfered) top end to hold the transformer. A 40-lb. bag of fast-setting posthole concrete will anchor it in place.

3 12-2 UF CABLE

4 LIGHT FIXTURES

2 THREADED SUPPORT STAKES

TYPICAL LOW-VOLTAGE LIGHTING SYSTEM

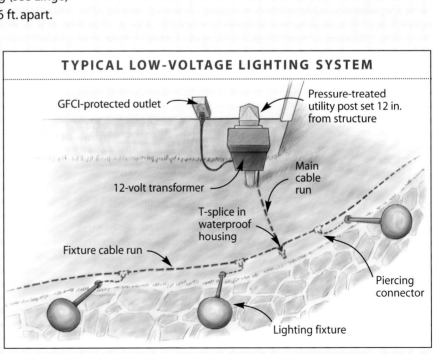

GFCI-protected outlet

Pressure-treated utility post set 12 in. from structure

12-volt transformer

Main cable run

T-splice in waterproof housing

Fixture cable run

Piercing connector

Lighting fixture

✚ WHAT CAN GO WRONG

A single outdoor outlet can serve all of your low-voltage lighting needs for this project, but code requires it to have a built-in ground-fault circuit interruptor (GFCI), which grounds the wires and cuts off the current in case of a short circuit to eliminate electrical shocks and surges.

Install the Transformer & Cable

1 **SET YOUR POST.** Using your narrow trench shovel, dig an 18-in.-deep, 12-in.-diameter hole within 12 in. of an exterior GFCI-rated outlet. Set a 3-ft.-long, pressure-treated 4×4 chamfered post into the hole, and fill the hole halfway with water. Use your level to keep the post plumb—perfectly upright—as you pour in the quick-setting concrete. Add water as the package directs, holding the post steady and plumb as the concretes sets.

2 **HOOK UP YOUR CABLE.** Use your wire cutters to divide the two strands of wire and allow 6 in. to 8 in. of slack. Strip back the plastic sheathing to expose about 1 in. of raw wire on each strand, then connect and tighten each to their respective hot and ground terminals on the transformer. Connect all of your cable and fixtures before you plug the transformer into the GFCI-rated wall outlet to avoid blowing the fuse or tripping the circuit breaker at the service panel.

3 **MOUNT THE TRANSFORMER ON THE UTILITY POST.** Measure the location of the mounting screws on the transformer and attach scrap 2×2 lumber to the utility post as brackets for the box. Mark and preset the mounting screws on the brackets so that the transformer's mounting holes slip onto the screws, then tighten the screws to secure the box to the post.

4 **EXCAVATE YOUR TRENCH AND LAY THE CABLE.** Before you do any digging, use a length of rope or garden hose to determine the contour of your trench, which will serve as a guide for its excavation. Using  your narrow trench shovel, remove the turf layer in as few pieces as possible and set it aside, then dig a trench for your cable, 18 in. deep and 3 in. wide. Lay the cable in the trench, uncoiling it as you go; make a 1-ft. loop at the location of each fixture, every 6 ft. along the trench. Coil any unused cable at the end of the trench as you place and hook up the light fixtures.

1 **2**

3 **4**

Protect the exposed ends of stripped and spliced wires with waterproof, gel-filled splice protectors. Buried with the cable, it keeps your splices dry while enabling a reliable and steady connection between the two wires.

⊘ **UPGRADE**

Make sure your 12-volt cable has 12-amp wires to reduce resistance in long runs and ensure that every lamp burns at the same brightness. Cables with 14-amp or 18-amp wires can cause lights at the end of a long strand to dim from electrical resistance as the current travels from the transformer to the light fixtures.

Attach the Lights

5 **SPACE OUT YOUR LIGHTS.** Use a retractable or reel tape measure to place your light fixtures 6 ft. apart along the trench. Backfill the trench and bury the main cable 4 in. deep, then place survey marker tape over the backfill to mark the location of your cable—a warning to anyone excavating near the trench in the future.

6 **MAKE THE TURN.** For this project, the trench took a right-angle turn so that the lights could follow a path. Always connect the transformer lead cable to the center of the lighting run, and use a T-splice to extend the fixture cable each way along the sidewalk. Remember to backfill and place survey marking tape over that section of cable as well.

7 **CONNECT YOUR FIXTURES.** For each light fixture, thread and attach the support stake, run the lead wire out of the hole provided, use the loop slack to position the fixture exactly, and connect the wire to the main cable using a piercing connector (see Cool Tool, p. 112). This quickly and easily connects the lead and main wires at each light fixture. Stake the fixture in the space between the trench and the path or sidewalk.

8 **TEST YOUR LIGHTS AND REPLACE THE TURF.**
Before you completely bury the cable, plug the transformer into the GFCI outlet and make sure every light comes on. Repair any that don't illuminate (typically from a bad bulb, faulty socket, or loose piercing connector). Backfill the trench, compact the dirt, and replace the turf so it lays flat and flush on the surface.

Set the timer on the transformer to automatically activate the lights, making sure the switch that controls the outlet, if any, is in the "on" position. Plug the transformer into the outlet and enjoy your yard day and night.

Illuminate the central path and the plants around the margin of your yard. Leave unlit areas of turf between the lights to make your yard appear to be larger.

Safety first is the watchword when it comes to steps and slopes in a path. Center-mounted light fixtures help you see the steps in the dark.

Low-voltage lighting offers a wide range of options to illuminate the features and functions of your yard. You can create dramatic shadows or highlight the rugged bark of a tree. You can also use lighting to direct attention to a focal point or destination— a gazebo or pond, for instance—by creating a line of sight with low-voltage lamps. Such perspective lighting schemes also make a small yard feel bigger.

Add artistic lighting fixtures of textured metal, blown glass, brass, and wrought iron.

Define different areas of your yard for maximum appeal. Spotlights on trees make them into night-time accents, and uplights on a stone wall or house draw attention to their textures.

Choose lights that are shielded when viewed from normal eye height. They cast their light downward, illuminating the ground beneath the fixture.

Avoid light fixtures that shine directly upward near paths and patios. The lights also should be tall enough to clear any flowers or shrubs beneath them.

Resources

ALLEN BLOCK® WALL SYSTEMS
5300 Edina Industrial Blvd.
Suite 100
Edina, MN 55439
(952) 835-5309
www.allanblock.com

BELGARD®
Walls & Floors for Your Outdoors©
OLDCASTLE ARCHITECTURAL, INC.
375 Northridge Rd., Ste. 250
Atlanta, GA 30350
(800) 899-8455
www.oldcastle.com

BRICKFORM®
RAFCO PRODUCTS
11061 Jersey Blvd.
Rancho Cucamonga, CA 92730
(800) 484-3399
www.brickform.com

G.I. DESIGNS
Decorative Landscape Lighting
700 Colorado Blvd., Suite 120
Denver, CO 80206
(877) 442-6773
www.gidesigns.com

NIGHTSCAPING
1705 East Colton Ave.
Redlands, CA 92374
(800) 544-4840
www.nightscaping.com

For more great weekend project ideas look for these and other
TAUNTON PRESS BOOKS wherever books are sold.

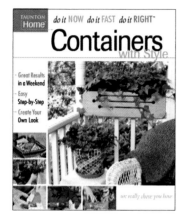

Containers with Style
1-56158-678-1
070760
$14.95

Paint Transformations
1-56158-670-6
070751
$14.95

Lighting Solutions
1-56158-669-2
070753
$14.95

Trim Transformations
1-56158-671-4
070752
$14.95

Storage Solutions
1-56158-668-4
070754
$14.95

For more information visit our Web site at www.doitnowfastright.com